School Accountability

The Hoover Institution gratefully acknowledges
the following individuals and foundations for their
significant support of the

Initiative
on
American Public Education

KORET FOUNDATION
TAD AND DIANNE TAUBE
LYNDE AND HARRY BRADLEY FOUNDATION
BOYD AND JILL SMITH
JACK AND MARY LOIS WHEATLEY
FRANKLIN AND CATHERINE JOHNSON
JERRY AND PATTI HUME
DORIS AND DONALD FISHER
BERNARD LEE SCHWARTZ FOUNDATION

*The Hoover Institution
gratefully acknowledges generous support from*

TAD AND DIANNE TAUBE
TAUBE FAMILY FOUNDATION
KORET FOUNDATION

*Founders of the program on
American Institutions and Economic Performance*

and Cornerstone gifts from
SARAH SCAIFE FOUNDATION

School Accountability

EDITED BY

Williamson M. Evers and Herbert J. Walberg

CONTRIBUTING AUTHORS

Williamson M. Evers

Chester E. Finn, Jr.

Eric A. Hanushek

Caroline M. Hoxby

Lance T. Izumi

Diane Ravitch

Margaret E. Raymond

Herbert J. Walberg

HOOVER INSTITUTION PRESS

STANFORD UNIVERSITY   STANFORD, CALIFORNIA

www.hoover.org

Hoover Institution Press Publication No. 512

First printing, 2002
07 06   9 8 7 6 5 4 3

Manufactured in the United States of America.

The paper used in this publication meets the minimum requirements
of the American National Standard for Information Sciences—
Permanence of Paper for Printed Library Materials, ANSI
Z39.48–1984.

Library of Congress Cataloging-in-Publication Data
School accountability / edited by Williamson M. Evers and
Herbert J. Walberg.
        p. cm. — (Hoover Institution Press publication ; 512)
"An assessment by the Koret Task Force on K–12 Education" —Cover.
Includes bibliographical references (p.) and index.
    ISBN 0-8179-3881-8 (alk. paper) — ISBN 0-8179-3882-6 (alk. paper)
    1. Educational accountability—United States. I. Evers, Williamson
M., 1948– II. Walberg, Herbert J., 1937– III. Koret Task Force on
K–12 Education. IV. Series.
    LB2806.22 .S36 2002
    379.1'58--dc21
                                            2002001172

Contents

Foreword

The Koret Task Force on K–12 Education—a joint endeavor of the Koret Foundation of San Francisco and the Hoover Institution—is a group of eleven education policy experts that seeks to evaluate the existing evidence on school reform measures and to conduct research on the quality and productivity of K–12 education in the United States. Immediately after the task force formally convened in 1999, its investment in research and writing began.

This venture is the conception of joint thinking between Tad Taube, president of the Koret Foundation, and myself. The Koret Foundation is a philanthropic organization that has decided to focus heavily on education issues in the United States. We both felt strongly that the Hoover Institution could contribute to the national dialogue on how to improve American public education. Thus, the Hoover Institution, with significant support from the Koret Foundation, embarked on a multiyear effort to identify and convey factual information about the state of American education, as well as to generate ideas that would enhance the opportunity for all children to gain more knowledge and assemble better skills.

The first book released by the Koret Task Force and edited by task force member Terry M. Moe, *A Primer on America's Schools* (Hoover Institution Press, 2001), cuts through the complexities and often unwarranted assumptions in the education debate and conveys essential information pertaining to this important public policy issue. In *A Primer on America's Schools*, this group takes an important step toward school reform by providing a broad overview of the current state of American education.

The *Primer* provided the foundation for the task force to proceed with two new projects on the important issues of school choice and accountability. These books are fresh contributions to a field that has become frozen by ideological disputes, bureaucratic resistance, and establishment views.

In *Choice with Equity*, edited by task force member Paul T. Hill, nine education specialists, including six members of the task force, take a hard look at the possible downsides of choice in education. These scholars ask whether choice is likely to increase student segregation by race and class or to harm students whose parents are not the first to choose a school. They acknowledge the risks inherent in poorly designed choice programs and suggest how choice can be structured to protect and actually benefit the disadvantaged.

In *School Accountability*, edited by task force members Williamson M. Evers and Herbert J. Walberg, scholars describe the present state of school accountability, how it evolved, how it succeeded and failed, and how it can best be improved. This book describes the range of efforts and identifies the best principles and practices that will improve accountability and hence our nation's schools.

I thank the task force members responsible for the design of these volumes and the editors and authors that contributed to it. I also thank the Koret Foundation for its continuing generous financial support that sustains the work of the task force, especially to Tad Taube for his help in creating the intellectual foundation for the task force and the Hoover Institution's Initiative on American Public Education.

The Koret Task Force on K–12 Education forms the centerpiece of the Hoover Institution's Initiative on American Public Education, with the overall goal of presenting pertinent facts surrounding the current debate, contributing to the debate as a constructive commentator, and generating new ideas relating to education reform. This is a multiyear commitment to the production of research and writing on education reform that citizens of the United States should be considering as a matter of public policy. We could not have launched this ambitious initiative without the help of the many individuals who have stepped forward to support this effort, many of whom are explicitly mentioned on the acknowledgment page.

John Raisian
Director
Hoover Institution

Introduction and Overview

Williamson M. Evers and Herbert J. Walberg

Although educators and school boards sometimes resist the idea, accountability is sorely needed in America's schools. This country's children are as able as children in other affluent, democratic nations, but they fall farther behind the longer they are in school, notwithstanding nearly the highest per-student costs.[1] In most instances, they make the least progress and wind up at or near the bottom of international rankings of achievement as they finish high school. Furthermore, a quarter century of numerous reforms, substantially more money, and rising student abilities has generally failed to raise achievement test scores.

Americans take great pride in the superior and ever-increasing effectiveness and efficiency of most of our industries. Yet our schools fall behind those in other countries and have become less rather than more efficient, which is far from what we would want, given their central importance in the American economy and society. School productivity or the relation of achievement to costs was 65 percent

---

[1]Herbert J. Walberg, "Achievement in American Schools," in *A Primer on America's Schools*, Terry M. Moe, editor, Stanford, CA: Hoover Institution Press, 2001.

higher in 1970–71 than in 1998–99.[2] Surveys of students, citizens, and employers, moreover, reveal substantial dissatisfaction with American schools.

If schools were doing well or even passably well, policymakers might be deservedly reluctant to insist on substantially greater accountability. Since schools are not doing well, however, the burden of proof in explaining this state of affairs should be on the present system. Yet the American K–12 system is distinctively unaccountable compared with other aspects of American life and compared with education systems in other countries. In the work world, for example, management and employees are held accountable. Those that do well gain merit raises, but in other cases, heads roll. The performance of sports and entertainment figures is closely measured, ranked, and encouraged through a variety of incentives. Firms, workers, athletes, and entertainers compete, and the marketplace creates incentives for their efficient performance, holds them closely accountable, and rewards success. The accountability principle extends to most sectors of American life; wise parents hold their children accountable for their behavior, and part of growing up is learning how to be self-accountable for one's ethics, ideals, and goals.

---

[2]Caroline M. Hoxby, "School Choice and School Productivity: (Or, Could School Choice be a Tide that Lifts All Boats?)," Washington, DC: National Bureau of Economic Research Conference on the Economics of School Choice, 2001. Professor Hoxby concluded as follows: "Consider the simplest productivity calculation, achievement per dollar, without any attempt to control for student characteristics. Such a calculation (which I describe in detail below) suggests that average public school productivity was about 65 percent higher in 1970–71 than in 1998–99. [If we] were simply to restore school productivity to its 1970–71 level, then the average student in the United States would be scoring at an advanced level where fewer than ten percent of students now score" (p. 2).

Contrary to many claims, higher education also shows poor achievement productivity. Alexander W. Astin, in "Undergraduate Achievement and Institutional Excellence" (*Science*, 1968, 161, 661–668), much extended in his *What Matters in College* (San Francisco, CA: Jossey-Bass, 1993), showed that wide variations in spending, facilities, library holdings, and similar costly inputs have no effect on value-added college and university achievement.

Compared to schools in other countries, those in the United States are subject to little accountability. The U.S. school system lacks the marketplace accountability of schools competing with one another and the further accountability of large-scale examination systems, both of which are associated with higher achievement.[3]

Educators' resistance to testing and accountability is not surprising and is rather to be expected. The essayist and playwright George Bernard Shaw said all professions are conspiracies against lay people. Neither doctors nor bricklayers would choose to be accountable for their efforts—it would be much easier for them to say that all's well as they request higher compensation.

Professional associations and unions have their members' interests and welfare as their first priority. So dealing with them in free society requires clients or consumers to represent and press for their own interests. In the case of schools, it is not unions but legislators, school boards, education leaders, taxpayers, and parents that have been remiss in failing to acquire information on the standings and efficiency of states, school districts, schools, and individual staff members.

Oddly, many educational psychologists and specialists in educational testing, evaluation, and statistics have been silent or reticent on the need for testing and accountability. Many, however, are in schools of education where views are unlike those in other walks of life. A recent Public Agenda survey of education professors showed that 64 percent think schools should avoid competition.[4] Education professors also differ from employers and other professionals on

---

[3]Ludger Woessmann, "Why Students in Some Countries Do Better," *Education Matters,* Summer 2001, 65–74.

[4]See Walberg, 2001. Nearly two-thirds of teacher educators admitted that education programs often fail to prepare candidates for teaching in the real world, and only 4 percent reported that their programs typically dismiss students found unsuitable for teaching. Thus, even starting with their undergraduate education, many prospective educators are laden with anticompetitive ideas against standards and incentives.

measuring standards or even employing them at all. Employers employ standardized examinations for hiring. So do selective colleges and graduate and professional schools for admission decisions. Such examinations are required in law, medicine, and other fields for licensing, in part because they are objective and reliable. Yet 78 percent of teacher educators wanted less reliance on objective examinations.

Even National Academy of Sciences (NAS) education committees, heavily populated by educators and education professors, have spoken out against tests and procedures designed to elevate educational standards and raise the stakes for success and failure. A recent NAS report, for example, warned against using scores from a single assessment for promoting students in school and retaining them in a grade for an additional year.[5]

The NAS committee failed, however, to point out adequately the advantages of relying on a single assessment. Using a single test is clear and definitive. It presents a challenge, which students and teachers have a strong incentive to meet. It has successful precedents in many fields, including K–12 schools outside the United States. Meeting standards in school is preparation for college, employment, sports, and other common endeavors where clear, objective, unambiguous standards are routine.

The NAS committee also neglected to point out adequately the harm that school systems, particularly those in big cities, have done to the careers of poor youth, who have not learned basic knowledge and skills, and the unfairness imposed on students capable of meeting higher standards, who have graduated with devalued diplomas because schools have not demanded high levels of achievement and have not tested to make sure those high levels have been attained.

---

[5]Jay P. Heubert and Robert M. Hauser, editors, *High Stakes: Testing for Tracking, Promotion, and Graduation,* Washington, DC: National Academy of Sciences, 1999. Fifteen of 25 members of the committee were school people and education professors.

The NAS committee held that tests should meet various stringent requirements before being used as criteria for high school graduation. Following their recommendations would be expensive, difficult, time-consuming, and unprecedented. Few states, perhaps none, have perfectly aligned their goals, standards, teaching materials, and tests with one another. Even if they did, frequent changes in one aspect may require changes in other aspects, making it extremely difficult to mount and maintain a system acceptable to the NAS committee.

Yet examinations with only "low stakes" consequences would mean a continuing escape from accountability for failing students, schools, and systems. There is justification, of course, for phasing in and elevating standards in measured steps, but there is little reason for retaining the present unproductive status quo until a perfect system can be devised.[6]

After a quarter-century of poor progress in educational productivity, the burden of proof is on schools rather than on tests per se or on the idea of accountability, and the time for inaugurating high standards and accountability is now. As common sense would suggest, moreover, research on standards and accountability shows their beneficial effects even in the many places where they have been put into effect in a far from ideal way.

Accountability critics, for example, maintained that strict Standards of Learning imposed on Virginia schools for accreditation would be a debacle. Instead, the percentage of schools meeting the standards rose from 2 percent to 40 percent from 1999 to 2001, and many more schools are expected soon to achieve the standards. Said State Superintendent of Education

---

[6]Without qualification, perfect alignment of lessons and test might mean "teaching to the test," which may risk trivializing both teaching and testing. Good tests usually rely on sampling of content, just as surveys rely on a small sample to estimate population views. They usually also avoid test items exactly like those in a textbook or class lesson so that students must master the application of principles to new or less familiar examples.

Jo Lynne DeMary, "In more and more schools, teachers and administrators are analyzing curricula and making the changes needed to improve instruction and increase student achievement."[7] Scholars have documented other impressive success stories.[8]

OVERVIEW

To analyze accountability issues, we have gathered a balanced set of contributions from authors who are specialists in studying education from the perspectives of the social and behavioral sciences: history, economics, political science, and psychology. These perspectives, sometimes combined in a single article, should enable readers to gain an understanding of what is known about accountability, what still needs to be learned, what should be done, and what is best avoided in devising accountability systems.

In the opening chapter, historian Diane Ravitch distinguishes policymakers' interest in results as measured by tests and reinforced by accountability mechanisms with professional educators' interest in improvement—possibly using tests for diagnostic purposes but not for accountability. The professional expects that spending more money in ways that professional educators like will yield improvement. Ravitch traces this view to the turn of the twentieth century when testing began to be used in college admissions. She carries her story through the Progressive era with its scientific and managerial ethos, in which testing was used in the hope of

---

[7]Alan Richard, "More Virginia Schools Hit Mark on Exams Used for Ratings," *Education Week,* October 24, 2001, pp. 26, 30.

[8]See subsequent chapters in this volume and Diane Ravitch (Editor), *Brookings Papers on Education Policy,* Washington, DC: Brookings Institution, 2001, particularly the chapters by Julian Betts and Robert Costrell; Herbert Walberg; Chester Finn and Marci Kanstoroom; David Grissmer and Ann Flanagan; and John Bishop, Ferran Mane, Michael Bishop, and Joan Moriarity, which summarize evidence that states that set clear standards, align curricula, publicize comparative results, and have begun incentive systems have made better than average achievement progress.

improving teaching practices and with the intent of fending off scrutiny from parents and taxpayers.

Policy analyst Chester E. Finn, Jr., uses the metaphor of the variegated pairings in the 1969 motion picture *Bob & Carol & Ted & Alice* to illuminate how choice and accountability work together. He finds that the best mixture combines choice (which he nicknames "Alice") among rival institutions, such as charter schools and voucher schools, with academic standards and external testing ("Ted"). Along the way, he reveals the flaws of other possible matches and mismatches of approaches.

For many years, economist Caroline Hoxby was a test skeptic because she thought that the benefits from testing (in the absence of accountability incentives) were too small to justify the cost. She has changed her mind. She finds that she had underestimated how much schools would improve to avoid being exposed as low performers, and she now realizes how inexpensive testing is. Hoxby calculates what testing actually costs, and she finds it to be one of the most cost-effective of all school reforms.

Economist Eric A. Hanushek and political scientist Margaret E. Raymond focus on incentives. They point out that, at present, most consequences fall on students; schools and teachers feel consequences only indirectly. Hanushek and Raymond describe the components of an effective accountability system. It should pinpoint where problems are and encourage appropriate change. They find, however, that knowledge of what works best in the classroom is still inadequate.

Policy analyst Lance T. Izumi and political scientist Williamson M. Evers analyze accountability in three states with comparatively strong systems: California, Texas, and Florida. Concentrating on a few states allows the authors to depict how accountability works in practice. They are most hopeful about the Florida system with its standards-based test, school report cards, merit pay for teachers, and exit vouchers for students in failing schools.

Psychologist Herbert J. Walberg points to the features needed in effective accountability systems and provides examples of consumer-friendly reporting of accountability results from actual accountability systems. Walberg contends that some of the existing tests and accountability systems are good enough to do the job and warns us not to let a yearning for perfection block implementation of approaches that will in fact work better than existing systems and continue to improve with experience.

These contributions from education policy specialists help us see how we came to have failing schools, low-performing students, and little accountability. They show how we can devise the affordable, reasonable, and workable accountability systems and incentives we need to raise student learning. Myths about accountability have misled some fair-minded people into fearing that accountability will somehow discourage learning. But in actuality, accountability and appropriate incentives offer our best hope for improving American public schools.

Testing and Accountability, Historically Considered

Diane Ravitch

Nowadays, one thinks of testing and accountability as twins in education; tests, it is assumed, produce the data on which accountability for results is based. However, as one surveys the history of American education, it quickly becomes clear that the history of testing is far more venerable than the history of accountability. Furthermore, history reveals a fundamental conflict between the education profession and laymen in the way they perceive the uses of testing and accountability. Much of the current controversy over testing and accountability can be traced to this conflict of perceptions.

Testing has long been a staple in American public education. Schools and colleges administered tests of various kinds in the nineteenth century and used them to limit promotion to the next grade and for college admission. But the contemporary idea of accountability, that is, holding not only students but also teachers, principals, schools, and even school districts accountable for student performance, is a recent invention. The idea of measuring the quality of education by the academic performance of students is not one with a long pedigree.

Nineteenth-century schools frequently tested their students to see if they had mastered what they were taught. Some tests were districtwide, whereas others were written by the teachers. The tests were very specific in terms of what they expected students to know; there was little room for ambiguity or nuance. Students who didn't pass the tests in history, geography, and arithmetic were "left back." They were held "accountable" if they failed to learn. In many school districts, students had to pass a test and/or complete a designated course of study in order to enter high school.

It was generally accepted by school officials and parents that enrollment in high school should be for those who could handle the work and that many youngsters either could not or did not want to do so. At the end of the nineteenth century, less than one of every ten adolescents went to high school. Those who wanted to enter high school were expected to demonstrate that they were ready. Most children left school at the end of eighth grade; either their families could not afford to keep them in school or they saw no reason to remain. Attendance was voluntary, and a high school diploma was not necessary for most kinds of work.

The small number of students who wanted to go to college had to prepare for college-level work. Many colleges accepted anyone who applied, but the most prestigious colleges required students to pass their admission examination. Elite colleges, such as Harvard, Princeton, and Yale, informed prospective students about the content of their examination, and students prepared to be examined by the college of their choice. Public and private secondary schools alike prepared their students for these college entry examinations. Many principals and headmasters complained about preparing students for different colleges (each with its own selections of reading from Latin authors). The volume of complaints inspired the creation in 1900 of the College Entrance Examination Board (CEEB), which prepared a single test of admission for a large number of colleges and allowed students to select the courses in which they would be examined.

Thus, those who wanted to go to a good public or private college knew that they would be held accountable for what they had learned. The establishment of the "College Boards" reinforced this expectation because the CEEB published its syllabus in different subjects, teachers taught it, and students were examined on whether they had mastered it.

School teachers in the nineteenth century were often required to pass a test of their knowledge, and often they were interviewed by members of the local school board. Oftentimes, the interview included a close examination of their religious views (the local school committee usually included members of the clergy) to make sure that the prospective teachers harbored no unconventional views. Once teachers were accepted for service, however, there were no more tests of their suitability or capacity. If their students failed to learn, it was the students' fault, and the students suffered the consequences of their ignorance or their lack of willpower by failing or by dropping out without graduating from high school.

The design and administration of testing began to change in the early years of the twentieth century after the field of educational psychology was established. As a new discipline, educational psychology found an institutional home in the new colleges of education and turned almost at once to the reform of educational testing. Most of the tests written by school districts and teachers were simple tests of recall; the psychologists criticized them for lacking reliability and validity. Their efforts to introduce scientific rigor into testing required standardization and adherence to psychometric principles of scientific objectivity.

The leading educational psychologist in the first half of the twentieth century was Edward L. Thorndike of Teachers College, Columbia University. Thorndike was determined to demonstrate that education could become an exact science; in his own research and in his textbooks, he stressed the importance of applying rigorous scientific methods to school practices. Thorndike eventually became known as the founding father of modern educational testing; he developed standard scales for testing pedagogical methods and school subjects.

Although Thorndike worked on perfecting tests as measures of academic performance, he had no interest in using testing for purposes of accountability. According to his biographer, Geraldine M. Joncich, Thorndike expected "that the high prestige of science would minimize outside interference, that the indisputability of scientific 'laws' would reserve educational control to educators trained in the principles and methods of a scientific pedagogy."[1] Like other progressives, Thorndike believed that education was a function of the state and that its administration should be a professional matter in which public oversight was strictly limited. By improving professional practice, Thorndike thought that there would be even less reason for noneducators to become involved in the operation of the public schools.

Thus, Thorndike's work on testing was intended to strengthen the profession, not to increase public oversight of the schools. He wanted to see teaching evolve from an art to a science; toward that end, he promulgated various "laws of learning." The Law of Exercise implied that children learned better when they practiced what they were supposed to learn. Thorndike's Law of Effect implied that children would learn better if the act of learning brought them a sense of pleasure or satisfaction. Progressive educators, who deeply admired Thorndike's intention to put education on a scientific footing, ignored the Law of Exercise, which smacked of rote recitation (which they despised), and applauded the Law of Effect, which supported child-centered schooling. In the child-centered school, the interest of the child was supposed to be the primary stimulus to learning,

---

[1]Geraldine M. Joncich, "Science: Touchstone for a New Age in Education," in *Psychology and the Science of Education: Selected Writings of Edward L. Thorndike*, New York: Teachers College Press, 1962, p. 7.

instead of the child's effort, and the Law of Effect suggested that children would not learn if they were required to engage in studies that they did not enjoy.

Led by psychologists like Thorndike, the testing movement evolved as the progressive education movement gained ideological dominance of the education profession in the 1930s and 1940s. Professional educators embraced testing because it seemed to place education on a scientific plane where decisions could be made on a professional basis and could withstand the entreaties of parents. Progressive educators were enamored of both child-centered practices and social efficiency; they sought to make the schools less academic and to create multiple programs for children who were not interested in traditional schooling. Tests, most especially intelligence tests, were used to sort children into different curriculum tracks so that the nonacademic students would be correctly placed into vocational and industrial programs. During the years of progressive hegemony, tests were extensively used for determining the aptitudes and intelligence of children and guiding them into the right curriculum track.

During the 1930s, as progressivism was in its heyday, the schools were encouraged by progressive leaders to promote children each year regardless of their performance. This practice came to be known as social promotion. At one level, it was a response to the Depression; it was intended to keep young people in school and out of the job market, thus reserving jobs for adults. But at another level, social promotion was championed by progressive educators who were concerned about the effects of retention and failure on the psychological well-being of the child. Advocates of social promotion insisted that schools should put less emphasis on subject matter, discipline, and grades and more emphasis on children's social adjustment.

Thus, although testing was regularly used in the schools, there was no belief within the profession that tests should be used to hold anyone accountable. The spread of social promotion meant that even students would not be held accountable for their performance in school. These trends were not reviewed by the public; no polls revealed whether parents wanted their children to be socially promoted. The transformation of the school from a meritocratic institution into a custodial institution happened almost entirely without public participation. These changes were facilitated by the profession's belief that the practice of education was strictly a professional matter that need not involve members of the public other than as taxpayers and by the development of a technical pedagogical lingo that made education seem to be near-incomprehensible to untutored laymen.

Interest in accountability may be traced to the landmark report *Equality of Educational Opportunity* of 1966, known as the Coleman report for its lead author, sociologist James Coleman. Written as a study to compare the distribution of resources and opportunities among children of different races, the Coleman report also examined differences in achievement scores, or outcomes. The study was significant for many reasons, one of which was its shift in research focus from inputs to results, which resulted from the authors' decision to examine how school resources affected achievement.[2]

Before the Coleman report, education reform had focused solely on the issue of resources, on the assumption that more generous provisions for teachers' salaries, facilities, textbooks, and supplies would fix whatever ailed the nation's schools. After the Coleman report, reformers advanced a broader array of proposals, many of which sought changes in performance rather than (or in addition to) increases in resources. In the late 1960s, some urban school systems experimented with decentralization or community control in an effort to shake up the bureaucratic structures that managed the schools. In 1971, the federal government sponsored a choice program in Alum Rock, California, which allowed

---

[2]Diane Ravitch, *The Troubled Crusade: American Education, 1945–1980,* New York: Basic Books, 1983, p. 168.

mainly low-income parents to choose among their district's public schools. During the same period, scores of school districts tried performance contracting with private firms to deliver remedial services to low-income students.

These tentative ventures into decentralization, choice programs, and privatization schemes resulted not from the demands of professional educators but because of the intervention of policymakers and local school boards. Professional educators continued to believe that the inadequacies of the schools could be resolved by adding additional resources. However, policymakers, public officials, and, in some cases, community activists and parents concluded that the problems were structural consequences of the bureaucratic system of public education and had to be addressed by competition or structural change.

The shift in focus from inputs (resources) to outputs (student achievement) was facilitated by the increased availability of test scores. The establishment of the National Assessment of Educational Progress (NAEP) in 1970 provided cumulative new data and trend lines to document the educational achievement of American students; after 1992, NAEP reporting was expanded to include samples of students in participating states. Another source of information about student achievement was contained in international tests of mathematics and science (the two subjects on which students in different nations may be compared); American students in grades eight and twelve, when international tests were usually given, often performed poorly and seldomly above the international mean.

As more and more information accumulated about student performance, elected officials came under pressure to "do something" about low achievement and about the large gaps among different groups of students: between those who were poor and middle-class and among students of different races. Confronted with the need to improve their schools in order to attract new industries to their states and localities, elected officials—especially governors—looked at education much as they looked at other functions of government and at private corporations. They concluded that what mattered most was results—that is, whether students were learning. They used test scores as the best measure of student learning, and they urged that schools should focus relentlessly on improving student achievement.

By the early 1980s, governors were turning to business leaders as their natural allies in trying to improve their state's educational system. In every state, education was the single biggest budget item, usually consuming 40 percent of the state's expenditures. Some governors wanted to get education under their control, some wanted to make education spending more cost-effective, and most wanted to accomplish both. The governors looked to business leaders for advice on managing complex, labor-intensive organizations. The business leaders looked at the schools through the lenses that were customary for them. They expected to see transparency of reporting about budget, resources, operations, and results; they expected to see accountability for performance. And they encouraged governors and other elected officials to consider incentive structures that worked routinely in business to improve performance.

Thus, over the past generation, a split has occurred between professional educators and the public officials who control the purse strings. In effect, there are two competing paradigms of education reform at work simultaneously and not always harmoniously. Professional educators and their allies in higher education continue to focus on inputs (resources for reducing class size, increasing teachers' salaries, and expanding teacher training, for example), whereas policymakers representing the public seek accountability for results.

If we accept the notion that there are two competing paradigms, then we can see how these paradigms are in constant tension, with advocates of first one, then the other, gaining brief advantage. Policymakers have sought accountability for students, teachers, schools, and school districts; professional educators have largely resisted these pressures. The grounds for their resistance have varied, depending on the issue, but in every instance the educators have sought to water down accountability and maintain professional discretion.

The policymakers want tests to have stakes for test-takers attached to them so that students will exert greater effort to pass them; the professional educators (with some notable exceptions) seek to soften and eliminate any stakes for students. The most notable exception to this generalization was Albert Shanker, who was president of the American Federation of Teachers until his death in 1996. Shanker advocated standards, testing, and stakes, and his union has mainly continued to follow his line; strong objections to stakes for students have been raised by the larger teachers' union, the National Education Association, as well as by other organizations of education administrators and researchers.

The policymakers have endorsed the standards-and-testing approach, in which states describe what students are expected to learn then test to see whether they have learned what they were presumably taught. Professional educators have gone along with this strategy with varying degrees of enthusiasm but with a chorus that warns about the danger that real incentives and sanctions will cause "teaching to the test," "narrowing the curriculum" to what is tested, and cheating by teachers.

The policymakers want to use test results to reward teachers with merit pay, on the assumption that teachers will respond to incentives for success, like participants in business organizations; the professional educators (or at least their unions) vigorously reject merit pay as a breach of professionalism that will undermine morale. The policymakers have endorsed transparent reporting of student performance, as opposed to norm-referenced reporting, so that parents can find out how their children are doing in relation to a meaningful standard. When the governing board of the National Assessment of Educational Progress authorized the creation of "achievement levels" (basic, proficient, advanced) in 1990 to replace norm-referenced proficiency scores, prominent members of the research community objected to the change (and continue to object) on mainly technical grounds.

Policymakers enacted laws in nearly forty states to permit the creation of public charter schools, hoping that their freedom from excessive government regulation would encourage higher performance. Educators were skeptical and, in some cases, openly objected to what they saw as a diversion of public funds to quasi-public (or quasi-private) schools.

Policymakers have supported the use of contracting to allow private companies to manage schools. Educators have seen this move as a threat to public education and, in some cases, have openly fought against the awarding of contracts to for-profit companies.

Policymakers have pushed for use of school report cards so that parents can find out how their children's schools are doing. They have also promoted the idea that failing schools would be subject to "reconstitution" (that is, reopening with a new staff and new principal), state intervention, and, in a worst-case scenario, a takeover of the school or school district by the state. None of these ideas emanated from educators, who continue to believe that the root problem of school failure is lack of resources.

The policymakers' pressure for accountability has not run into a brick wall of resistance. It would be more accurate to say that it has plunged into a bowl of Jell-O™, in which demands for accountability are eventually but inevitably transformed into demands for more resources. Educators want to improve student performance, but to do so they must have higher salaries, smaller class sizes, more training, and so on. The starkest illustration of this transaction can be found in Massachusetts, which passed an ambitious school reform law in 1993. As part of the plan, the state pledged to put up an extra one billion dollars every year, on the understanding that students would be expected to pass state examinations for high school graduation by 2003. The state did put up the money it promised, but by 2000, many educators were in revolt against the state testing program. The state's teacher union even ran an expensive advertising campaign and sponsored legislation to roll back the implementation of the state graduation tests.

Perhaps the most intriguing aspect of the debate over standards and accountability is that the states that have persisted in this strategy over time have seen steady improvement in student performance. North Carolina, Massachusetts, and Texas saw strong achievement gains for their students, both on state tests and on the regular tests administered by NAEP. The gains were especially significant for black and Hispanic students, whose performance in all states lagged far behind their white and Asian peers. In Virginia, which set high standards and aligned their state tests to those standards, the initial results were nothing short of appalling. But by the third year of testing, as teachers became familiar with the state's curriculum and as schools took accountability seriously, student performance was racheted up. In 1998, for example, the first year that the state tests were administered, only 40 percent of students passed the Algebra I test; by 2001, the proportion who passed had grown to 74 percent. Here, too, African American students made steady test-score gains.

As policymakers and educators jousted over the fate of accountability programs, another version of accountability lurked on the sidelines: vouchers. The theory of vouchers was that marketplace accountability would cure the ills of the schools; with sufficient information and the freedom to choose, went the theory, parents would withdraw their children from poor schools and send them to better schools. Public school leaders and teachers' unions railed against vouchers; they charged that they were unconstitutional because parents might use public funds to send their children to religious schools and warned that vouchers would destroy public education by allowing the most motivated families to flee to private and religious schools.

Vouchers directly challenge the supremacy of the state system of public education, so it is not surprising that spokesmen for public education would vigorously attack them. Vouchers are a form of accountability because they offer parents the opportunity to exit an institution that does not satisfy them. This is an alarming promise to professionals whose livelihood is dependent on the survival of that institution.

Thus far, the political battles over vouchers have limited the implementation of this policy initiative to only two cities (Milwaukee and Cleveland) and one state (Florida). The Democratic party is strongly allied to the teachers' unions, is completely opposed to vouchers in any form, and can barely countenance even public school choice. The Republican Party is ideologically sympathetic to vouchers because its preference for the free market predisposes it to embrace market solutions to social problems. But the Republican Party is irresolute about vouchers because the issue has a weak base within the Republican Party: rural districts don't care about school choice, as they ordinarily have only a few schools in their district; suburban districts are not animated about school choice because their students' performance is usually above the state's average; urban districts, where student performance and graduation rates are low, rarely vote Republican. So, even though there is strong support among young African Americans and Hispanic Americans for various forms of school choice, these groups vote reliably Democratic and do not exert any political pressure for a reform they prefer.

There will continue to be clashes between the policymakers who seek accountability and the educators who seek to deflect it. We can expect to see policymakers pumping more resources into education with the expectation that more inputs will eventually produce better outcomes for students. To some extent, this is a reasonable assumption: teacher salaries should be high enough to attract well-educated college graduates into the classroom; school facilities should be ample; school supplies should be adequate to students' needs;

and teachers should get additional education to stay abreast of improved methods and knowledge.

We can also expect that demands for improved performance will not abate. The public will continue to insist that students should be able to read, write, use mathematics, and be generally well prepared for further education or for technical jobs when they graduate high school. If large numbers of students continue to be poorly prepared, the public is likely to conclude either that a generation of school reform has failed or that the reforms to date have been too timid. If that should happen, then interest in accountability through market reforms—that is, vouchers—is likely to have greater public support than it has until now. Albert Shanker presciently recognized that the failure of standards-based reforms might pave the way for market-based reforms. His premature death, however, canceled out the one prominent voice among professional educators who was ready to lead a campaign in support of a strategy of standards, testing, and accountability.

In the near term, American education will continue to be driven by the two paradigms: the professional education paradigm, which deeply believes that the profession should be insulated from public pressure for accountability and which is deeply suspicious of the intervention of policymakers; and the policymaker paradigm, which insists that the public school system must be subject to the same incentives and sanctions based on its performance as are other large-scale organizations. How this conflict is resolved, and whether it is mooted by technological change in the delivery of education in the next decade or two, will determine the future of American education.

Real Accountability in K–12 Education
The Marriage of Ted and Alice

Chester E. Finn, Jr.

"Accountability" could be the most-used word in contemporary American educational parlance, but it may also have the most nebulous and multifarious meaning. Indeed, the term now faintly recalls the late-sixties drama *Bob & Carol & Ted & Alice*, for it has four main characters and they couple, bicker, fight, and generally interact in almost every imaginable combination. Each has problems. Some combinations tend to fight, whereas others make beautiful music together, at least some of the time.

This paper introduces and appraises the four versions of accountability that are most important to education reform in today's United States, together with some of the combinations, tensions, and confusions that arise among them. It examines how they work in the charter school context. It concludes by suggesting that the most promising accountability strategy for the future—albeit no sure thing—entails a judicious, charterlike combination of two versions. This can be thought of as the marriage of Ted and Alice but with a carefully drawn antenuptial agreement.

First, let us meet the quartet.

1. *Compliance.* "Trust the system" (Bob). Follow its rules and procedures. Generally work within—and seek to improve—that system. Put emphasis on whether everything is done according to the rulebook and whether resources are adequate and properly deployed. If there's a problem, change or add a rule, a program, a procedure, or a person. Continually fiddle with the inputs. If kids aren't learning enough, give them more teachers, more course requirements, more homework, or additional computers. This is classic bureaucratic accountability, hierarchical, top-down, and regulatory. It's so familiar we don't ordinarily even think of it as accountability. Although today it's apt to include rhetoric about results, in fact what participants in the enterprise are chiefly accountable for is obeying instructions and managing inputs and processes.

2. *Professional norms and expertise.* "Trust the experts" (Carol). This is also a within-the-system form of accountability, but its dynamics are different. As in medicine, law, or the clergy, its main force comes from deference to what one's professional peers and colleagues deem the truest or best way to do things. Though devotees of Carol-style professional accountability may also pay lip service to bureaucratic (Bob-style) compliance, to serving clients (Alice), and to meeting standards (Ted), the main focus is on, say, teaching math as recommended by the National Council of Teachers of Mathematics or having one's college of education accredited by the National Council on Accreditation of Teacher Education (NCATE) or selecting superior teachers through the National Board for Professional Teaching Standards (NBPTS) or ensuring that one's school faithfully embodies the "Multiple Intelligences" theory of learning. Such reference groups are privately organized, so they're not officially in charge of one's actions (though some, such as NCATE and NBPTS, wheedle their way into state policy and become

virtual arms of the bureaucratic system) and their sources of influence have mainly to do with the creeds, gurus, and belief structures of the educational profession. Indeed, it's not wrong to see Carol-style accountability as akin to joining a devout religious sect and holding oneself to the tenets of that sect. Like any true believers, people who feel primarily accountable to their professional peers are apt to pay only grudging attention to consumer preferences, to policies set by elected lay bodies, and to bureaucratic control systems. They'll do what they must in those accountability domains but only for pragmatic reasons. Their private conversation often dwells on how to surmount some hurdle that outsiders have placed in the path of true professionalism.

3. *Standards-based reform.* "Trust, but verify" (Ted). This is probably the most discussed form of accountability today, certainly in policy (and business) circles. It's what gets the spotlight at national "summits" and in legislative chambers. Think of it as a top-down, externally imposed strategy for inducing change in education by stipulating what children are supposed to learn in school, testing to see whether they've learned it, and imposing consequences on children (and sometimes adults) depending on how well it's been learned. The essential mechanisms are these: some higher level of political authority—most often a legislature or state board of education, nearly always an entity outside the educational profession proper—develops academic standards that a child, classroom, school, school system, or entire state is supposed to attain. That same higher authority also imposes tests or other measures by which to determine whether and how well its standards are being met. A fully wrought accountability system then dispenses rewards and sanctions (or interventions) meant to change behavior down the line and thereby to foster improved results. Until recently, most people thought of standards-based reform as driven chiefly by states, and, for the most part, that remains true. Today, however, in the aftermath of Bill Clinton's Goals 2000 program

and George W. Bush's "no child left behind" proposal, we're accustomed to Uncle Sam at least trying to push states, districts, and schools toward standards-based accountability.

4. *The marketplace.* "Trust the customers" (Alice). The fourth and final member of our accountability quartet grew up outside the traditional public school system in the company of schools that are directly answerable to their clients through market dynamics. Private schools, for example, must satisfy their customers, not only with respect to academics but in a hundred other ways as well, or they risk losing enrollment and revenue. Charter schools face a similar situation. Only if they can attract and keep students will they have income. What could more forcefully concentrate the mind?

Market-style accountability has spread beyond private and charter schools to include sundry forms of public school choice, "virtual" schooling, "magnet" schools, and vouchers—both the publicly and privately financed kinds. It remains, however, the most controversial of these four strategies, for it's the only one that employs a flexible definition of public education and that—in some versions— allows tax-generated monies to flow into schools not directly controlled by governmental bodies. Note, though, that it's not the only strategy that defers to private norms and values. As we have seen, professional (i.e., Carol-style) accountability is also characterized by deference to the views of nongovernmental groups and entities.

COMBOS

These four forms of accountability are not mutually exclusive. Indeed, it's unusual to find a school where only one of them is operating. Here are the most common combinations:

Bob and Carol. This is the longest-established and most frequent coupling: bureaucratic compliance plus professional norms. It's the accountability package that operates— to the extent that anything does—in most conventional U.S. public schools (and many other lands). A school's principal, for example, leads a staff that was chosen (and compensated, and tenured) by the system's central office, but it's his job to whip them into a school team that honors the precepts of, say, the Coalition of Essential Schools or that teaches reading according to the dictates of the International Reading Association.

Bob and Ted. Over the past decade, this has also become a commonplace pairing: bureaucratic compliance plus standards-based reform. In this combination, the standards-based part, which is top-down in its own right, melds with old-fashioned management of inputs and practices. From the school's standpoint, instead of simply complying with rules and procedures about resources and programs, the staff must now also fulfill externally imposed standards and produce externally mandated results. The combination tends to make for a docile staff, and maybe also a cynical one, as it doesn't take huge imagination to see that Bob-style compliance rules governing inputs and services can easily get in the way of Ted-style demands for improved test scores. (Consider, for example, a special-education regulation that keeps a disruptive child in the classroom of a harried teacher who then has less time to ensure that the other twenty-three kids learn how to multiply and divide.)

Carol and Ted. This combo may make more sense on paper than in reality, but it's far from unusual: professional norms *cum* standards-based accountability. Recall how the NCTM math standards have been folded into the standards-based reforms of many states. Picture an achievement-minded district prodding its schools to embrace designs developed under the auspices of New American Schools. A school that is striving to install, say, the "Roots and Wings" program is almost surely doing so in order to meet higher state or district standards. Conversely, a district that reconstitutes a school because it has failed to attain standards will likely use a "professional" design as part of the involuntary makeover.

Carol and Alice. This couple, too, can be spotted together more often as new schools of choice (charters, especially, but also outsourced schools) model themselves on professional school designs and standards. A charter school application that recently crossed my desk, for example, pledged that the new school would follow Howard Gardner's theory of "Multiple Intelligences." In Colorado, many new charter schools employ the "Core Knowledge" curriculum developed by E. D. Hirsch. As for the management firm now called Edison Schools, not only does it have a professionally crafted school design of its own, but also within that design is another: the "Success for All" program for primary reading.

The remaining two of the six duos are rare. We will return to Ted and Alice (standards plus marketplace) because I believe that couple holds great promise for education accountability in the United States. As for Bob and Alice, theirs is an uncommon and fundamentally incompatible pairing: bureaucratic compliance cum marketplace dynamics. The only situation where one is apt to find it struggling to work is where the system mandates that school choices be provided—such as a centrally created set of magnet schools, perhaps for purposes of racial integration. But it seldom succeeds, for the essence of top-down management militates against the free play of market dynamics. It's tough for a school's principal to follow the superintendent's dictates in core domains such as staffing, budget, and curriculum while also holding her school accountable for satisfying its clients.

The ménage-a-trois is infrequent but not unheard of, although, as is usual in such relationships, the situation may be unstable and the three participants may not be full equals. Bob, Carol, and Ted are the most apt to join together in a melding of bureaucratic compliance, professional norms, and external standards. Indeed, many education reformers think this is a strong trio. It's where one finds a school system in hot pursuit of state standards mandating that certain professionally approved reforms be put in place, such as extra pay for NBPTS-certified teachers or compulsory participation in specific staff-development programs or installation of the Modern Red Schoolhouse design in a faltering Title I school.

Of the other three possible trios, the only one that doesn't include the hapless pairing of Bob (compliance) and Alice (markets) is the combination of Carol, Ted, and Alice: professional norms plus standards plus market forces. This can be a jolly group, but I see it as a refinement upon the Ted and Alice duo and will discuss it briefly in that context.

As we've seen, many combinations within the quartet of accountability strategies can be imagined, and some are often encountered in the real world of K–12 schooling. But we've also seen some basic incompatibilities, especially where Bob (compliance) and Alice (markets) are involved. Carol (experts) is a bit of a loner at heart, not entirely happy keeping company with *any* of the others because they invariably mean accommodating forces outside the profession. That she has to do this all the time doesn't mean she likes it. Alice has a go-it-alone tendency, too, inclined to believe that the marketplace is all-knowing and can be counted upon to confer the greatest good upon the greatest number without help from other forces. As for compliance-minded Bob, he's such a control freak that he'll keep company with anyone he suspects he has a chance of bending to his will. Ted (standards), though, is a pretty versatile guy who, under the right circumstances, can get along with any of the others. So long as one is relaxed about who sets the standards, what forms the rewards and interventions take, and who monitors and enforces success, standards-based reform can cohabit with any of the other three.

DECIDING WHICH IS BEST

In light of all these options, how is the perplexed policy-maker to map a clear path toward a sound accountability system for his state or community? He might begin by setting some basic criteria. Four are key:

1. Which accountability strategy focuses most directly on academic achievement?

2. Which is most apt to work effectively (i.e., to produce the desired results)?

3. Which is most amenable to implementation?

4. Which brings the greatest problems and the most negative baggage?

Let's take these up in turn. For simplicity, we'll avoid couples and trios and instead just review the four individual strategies against these criteria.

WHICH IS FOCUSED MOST DIRECTLY ON ACADEMIC ACHIEVEMENT?

Ted has got to be the winner here. Standards-based reform arose because of the need to focus education dynamics on stronger achievement among students. If Bob (compliance) or Carol (experts)—the older members of the quartet—had done a good job of accomplishing that, Ted (standards) likely would never have come along. As for Alice (markets), she concentrates on achievement to the extent that it matters to parents and other consumers. One might hope that's most of the time, although we know it's not always their foremost concern.

WHICH IS MOST APT TO PRODUCE THE DESIRED RESULTS?

This depends, of course, on what results are sought and how much confidence one has that bureaucratic compliance or professional norms will accomplish this. If we stick with improved student achievement as the chief objective, I hold out scant hope for Bob (compliance) and not much more for Carol (experts), at least not while her professional norms have more to do with beliefs and ideologies than with hard evidence about effective school designs, curricula, and instructional methods. Ted (standards) has begun to prove himself in a few places—perhaps most famously in Texas and North Carolina, as well as some districts and a number of other countries—but (as we'll see below) it's hard to implement standards-based reform. As for Alice (markets), there's plenty of evidence that private schools do a pretty good job both of producing relatively high-achieving students and of satisfying their clients. There's mixed evidence with respect to charter schools, most of which are still new. And there's conflicting evidence about voucher programs, although I'm persuaded by Peterson's work that black youngsters benefit from them.[1]

WHICH IS MOST AMENABLE TO IMPLEMENTATION?

Bob's approach is relatively easy to implement—schools and local, state, and federal education agencies have been in a compliance mode for decades—but he isn't very successful at producing superior results. That's largely due to the fact that education is a field where manipulating inputs does not reliably translate into stronger outcomes. For example, tightening teacher certification requirements, installing additional courses and technology, or reducing class sizes only intermittently yields better student achievement. A further problem is that the successful implementation of one compliance scheme may interfere with the next: those tighter certification requirements, for instance, are apt to make it harder to ensure that a fully certified teacher leads every classroom. So are uniform salary schedules that require high school physics

---

[1]See, for example, William G. Howell, Patrick J. Wolf, Paul E. Peterson, and David E. Campbell, "Vouchers in New York, Dayton, and D.C.," *Education Matters,* vol. 1, no. 2, Summer 2001.

teachers to be paid the same as middle school social studies instructors.

Carol (experts) has always had implementation problems in public education, mainly because "the profession" is almost never fully in charge of key decisions, actions, and resources. Those NCTM math standards, for instance, may be well implemented and yet not do a very good job of preparing kids to pass the state math test if the latter is aligned with a different view of math (or not aligned at all). Even where NCATE gets its accreditation required for teacher training programs to win state approval, the legislature may also create an "alternative" certification scheme that bypasses those training programs altogether.

Ted (standards) is proving hard to implement successfully in many places. It's difficult to reach agreement on standards, hard to get the assessments properly aligned with those standards, and painful—mainly for political reasons—to impose meaningful consequences on students, teachers, and schools. Where these challenges have been met (again, in places like Texas), Ted seems to work pretty well. But a great many states are tangled in their knickers when it comes to standards-based reform. They find it politically difficult to resist the many temptations to compromise standards, which can be done through more devices than most reform-watchers realize, some of them none too visible. First, most conspicuous are a state's formal academic standards, which are widely available and much examined.[2] These can be strong or weak, easy or exacting. Second is the quality and rigor of the state test, which is supposed to conform to the published academic standards but often does not. Third is

[2]The Thomas B. Fordham Foundation and I have done our share of this. See, for example, Chester E. Finn, Jr., and Michael J. Petrilli, *The State of State Standards 2000,* Washington DC: Thomas B. Fordham Foundation, January 2000. See also Chester E. Finn, Jr., and Marci Kanstoroom, "State Academic Standards," in *Brookings Papers on Education Policy 2001,* Diane Ravitch, editor, Washington DC: Brookings Institution Press, 2001.

where to set the cut-off or passing score on that test. (It's possible to have a test that contains plenty of challenging questions but then deem students to have passed it even though they answer few of those questions correctly.) Fourth and finally comes the low-visibility but high-impact decision as to how many of the students in a school must pass the test in order for the school itself to be judged successful. With so many ways to let standards slip, it is little wonder that we find many states reporting far larger fractions of their students (or schools) being deemed proficient on the states' own measures than are judged proficient according to the standards set by the National Assessment Governing Board (NAGB) for reporting results on the National Assessment of Educational Progress (NAEP).[3] And even when a state holds firm in its standards, it may falter in the politically ticklish task of attaching rewards and sanctions to student, school, and teacher performance.

Alice encounters big political obstacles because the marketplace approach threatens the traditional interests and power structures of public education. It can also be difficult to design the right ground rules for such a system. Practically nobody favors a completely unfettered marketplace with zero policy involvement on behalf of the public interest. (Well, a tiny band of libertarians does.) But the policy questions quickly grow as intricate as the politics. For example, should children from wealthy families get the same vouchers as do children from poor families? What about disabled kids? Youngsters already enrolled in private schools? Should charter schools be funded on exactly the same basis as regular public schools? Which regulations should they not be

---

[3]For an early explanation of this phenomenon, see Mark D. Musick, "Setting Education Standards High Enough," Southern Regional Education Board: July 1996. Musick found that in twelve of thirteen states that he examined, a substantially larger fraction of eighth graders were said to meet their states' math proficiency standard in 1994–95 than scored at (above) the "proficient" level on the NAEP math assessments of 1992 and 1996.

exempted from? What rules should govern the boards and universities that "sponsor" charter schools? In what ways are *they* accountable?

Which System Carries the Most Negative Baggage?

The answer naturally depends upon one's values, as what appears bleak to one policymaker can look rosy to another. Measured simply in terms of controversy, Ted (standards) and Alice (markets) cause the most trouble. They're the newest and least familiar. Because they both emphasize outside-the-system accountability, they are especially objectionable to traditional education interests and dogmatists. Alice's marketplace strategy carries the added burden of seeming to cater to "private" interests. On the other hand, Bob (compliance) and Carol (experts) bring problems of their own, notably the fact that they're largely discredited in the eyes of governors, business leaders, and others outside the system who are pressing for stronger student achievement, more productive schools, and more effective educators.

WHAT CAN WE LEARN FROM CHARTER SCHOOLS?

Being relatively new and contentious, Ted (standards) and Alice (markets) not only have to prove themselves separately but also have to demonstrate that they can get along together. Though both come from "outside the system," they follow different theories and many people believe they are incompatible. After all, standards-based reform is top-down, driven by elites that tell schools what results to achieve—and reward and punish them. Market-style reform is populist and bottom-up, relying on the preferences of clients to signal to schools what must be done and on the individual actions of schools and educators to satisfy those clients.

In today's education policy tussles, Ted (standards) and Alice (markets) each have many fans and partisans, but their advocates tend to be leery of one another. Advocates of the marketplace don't think a dirigist, state-run accountability system can ever work well, whereas cheerleaders for "systemic reform" doubt that markets will be good for schools, children, or the common weal.

The closest thing we have to a test case is charter schools. They are where we can most easily observe Ted (standards) and Alice (markets) cohabiting. These independent public schools of choice must answer to their customers via the marketplace or they cannot count on continuing. But because they are a genre of public schools, they are also answerable to government and accountable for fulfilling the terms of their charters, which are typically issued and monitored by some public authority (usually a state or local school board, sometimes a state university) and which nearly always incorporate the state's academic standards and tests as part of a school's accountability mechanism.

Charter schools, in other words, must answer in both directions: to Ted, for meeting the state's academic standards (or whatever standards are written into their contracts), and to Alice (i.e., to their client marketplace). In the real world, they are also accountable in sundry ways to colleges, employers, accrediting bodies, curriculum developers, athletic leagues, health departments, and so on. They never escape entirely from Bob's compliance regimen—they're subject to special-education rules, for example—and occasionally they're also subject to union contracts. But for the most part these schools are self-guided and free from much conventional red tape. Hence it's possible for many of them to get beyond external accountability and begin to develop elements of what Paul Hill and colleagues term "internal accountability," defined as "the ways the school leadership and staff work together on a day-to-day basis to ensure that the school works for students and is therefore able to keep its promises to others."[4] This can also be seen as a special form of Carol-style professional accountability, one that's more internally than externally referential.

The experience of charter schools suggests that Ted (standards) and Alice (markets) can live together under the same roof, although a school may feel some tension between them. For example, "upward" accountability for academic achievement might argue for hiring another math teacher or reading specialist so as to boost those test scores; but from the clients' standpoint it may be more urgent for the school to replace its gym teacher, fix the rest room, or improve its before- and after-care offerings. Considering the limited resources of most charter schools, these trade-offs can be painful.

How well is charter school accountability actually working—and how sound a model does it offer the larger K–12 enterprise? There are signs that it's working better than most, although we cannot yet know how it will do over the long haul.

Certainly the great majority of students and parents (and teachers) in charter schools are satisfied with them—and pleased to have made the change. Demand generally outstrips supply, both on the part of families (and staff) seeking places in existing charter schools and on the part of would-be charter operators seeking to launch schools (but often deterred by politically-imposed caps and lean fiscal rations). Market signs, in short, indicate that charters are satisfying their clients and participants. Another hopeful sign on the charter accountability front, though in somewhat backwards fashion, is the fact that eighty-plus of these schools have shut down or have been shut down. Some could not attract or keep students; in other words, market-style accountability

---

[4]Paul Hill, Robin Lake, et al., "Charter School Accountability," Office of Educational Research and Improvement, U.S. Department of Education, June 2001, <http://www.ed.gov/pubs/chartacct>, p. 13.

(Alice) closed them. Others ran into fiscal difficulties—occasionally corruption and illegality—that led their sponsor to pull the plug (i.e., Bob-style accountability). A very few have been closed due to academic (i.e., Ted-style) shortcomings. This brings us to the big unanswered question of charter accountability: whether they're producing the requisite academic results. So far, the most we can say is that some are and some aren't. The data from several states are encouraging; others are gloomier. Schools that have been around longer—and whose students have been enrolled longer—seem more effective than new ones. But with the average U.S. charter school barely two years old, the most that can be said is that it's too soon to be sure.[5]

TAKING STOCK

What we really learn from observing charter schools is that they help us see the frailties and idiosyncrasies of the entire school-accountability enterprise. We learn that the top-down, standards-based version is only as good as the quality of a state's standards and tests and the conscientiousness, wisdom, and toughness of a school's sponsor. If Bob (compliance) and Ted (standards) are both in fine fettle, knowing what to demand and when to be lenient and possessing clear standards and sound indicators of performance, this can work very well indeed. If Carol (experts) is also in good shape, a charter school will honor the curricular, pedagogical, and philosophical values of a well-conceived and thoroughly researched program and will shun silly fads and ideologically driven practices. As for the marketplace side of charter accountability—Alice's territory—that works well, too, so long as Alice is thriving—so long, that is, as the school is transparent; its clients are well informed, fussy

---

[5]For an extended discussion, see Chester E. Finn, Jr., Bruno V. Manno, and Gregg Vanourek, *Charter Schools in Action*, Princeton: Princeton University Press, 2000.

(without being outrageous), and reasonably sophisticated; and enough decent school alternatives are available to them that their local education marketplace is vibrant with supply as well as demand.

The problem is that all four members of the accountability quartet can misbehave as badly with respect to charters as with conventional schools. Hanging a charter sign over the door doesn't immunize a school from accountability hazards. Bob (compliance) is a tireless control freak who exerts his authority more than he should, grabs for the rulebook whenever he can, and likes nothing better than to close loopholes that afford some schools more freedom than others. Carol (experts), as we have seen, has a loony streak, and charter schools are not always free from her daffier beliefs and practices. Ted (standards) has difficulty getting his standards right and his tests aligned. And Alice (markets) deserves a better education marketplace than she often finds herself working in. Even in the charter world, we find producers that are secretive with important consumer information, we find a dearth of viable school options, and we encounter families that care more about a school's convenience and amenities than its academic quality.

Now we've reached the central dilemma of school accountability. *None* of these approaches is idiot-proof. None is immune to bad ideas, distorted priorities, inept management, and old-fashioned laziness. Every one of them hinges on the sagacity, competence, integrity, and determination of those running it—no matter whether that's a governor or a parent. Each also depends for its success upon the creation of a reasonably consistent and fair system—think of this as the school accountability equivalent of the "rule of law"—rather than one that's quixotic, unpredictable, and prey to favoritism and politics. Yet the ground rules of all such systems depend in turn upon the wisdom, public-mindedness, and deftness of the policymakers who determine how they operate. (Yes, that's even true of the marketplace. Consider how a law limiting each community to two charter schools dampens supply; consider, too, how dependent charter clients are on state-generated test data.)

So what to do? If none of the four characters in our little accountability drama is perfect, and yet we must somehow persevere, what's our best option?

The *worst* idea is to turn back to Bob (compliance) and Carol (experts). They had many decades to show that compliance and professionalism would produce solid results in U.S. elementary and secondary schools, and they failed miserably. So let's not persist any longer in pretending that the accountability secret rests with them.

I believe the prospect of success is brightest in the union of Ted and Alice (i.e., the intersection of standards-based, top-down accountability and market-style, bottom-up accountability, much as we have seen operating in the charter world). This combination doesn't operate flawlessly in the case of charter schools, to be sure. But it's superior to the available alternatives and worth trying to perfect.

In suggesting that we rely on *both* Ted and Alice, I contend that the couple is more powerful than either of its members alone. This is a point worth pausing on, for the very thought that they can coexist, much less that they can strengthen one another, will come as news to people who have come to regard these two forms of accountability as rival superpowers locked in a cold war for control of American education.

It's no secret that most devotees of top-down reform are cool toward the marketplace approach. They regard it as messy, uncertain, divisive, apt to leave the neediest children behind, and too tolerant of ill-conceived schools. But the converse is also true. Many market aficionados are wary of universal, big-government schemes, especially in education, where they've seen standards-based reform founder on the shoals of political correctness, unproven education theories, political cowardice, and dubious psychometric assumptions. Hence factions have emerged. Most people who care about these things have joined one side or the other. For them, accountability is inseparable from their preferred reform strategy—and the other approach is suspect if not feared.

We've already looked at charter schools as evidence that these two systems can co-exist. It's worth noting one other prominent example. Florida has devised a standards-based accountability system that uses exposure to the marketplace as the ultimate "consequence" that can befall a failing school. That makes Florida the only place in America that has purposefully sought to harness the two forms of accountability in a comprehensive statewide system. (President Bush proposed something similar for the big federal Title I program, but Congress nixed most of it, including the school-choice component.) Enacted in 1999, Florida's "A+" plan assigns a letter grade to every public school in the Sunshine State based primarily on the school's performance on statewide tests. If a school gets an "F" for two years (out of four), its students become eligible for vouchers (i.e., can take their state dollars to the schools of their choice, including private and parochial schools).

So far, that stark fate has only befallen two Florida schools, and even they managed to crawl up to the "D" level the following year. (It is alleged by some that Florida has eased its grading standards for schools.) Nor did every pupil in those two schools opt to enroll elsewhere. Thus, only about fifty Florida youngsters have actually used vouchers to change schools via the state accountability program. Still, the "A+" design illustrates one way of yoking top-down, standards-based accountability to the marketplace kind— and suggests that the union of Ted (standards) and Alice (markets) is not limited to charter schools. Florida's approach is sometimes termed "exit vouchers" because it enables youngsters to escape from low-performing schools into the wider education marketplace.

This, too, is controversial. Anything that takes kids or dollars out of public schools (no matter how crummy) is inherently contentious. That's why Congress would not assent to exit vouchers at the national level. Yet at least one analyst who has examined the Florida program judges that it was precisely the threat of vouchers that caused the state's failing public schools to tug hard on their own bootstraps.[6] In other words, exposure to the marketplace—even a whiff of the marketplace—is an action-forcing consequence that can play a dynamic and constructive role within a regimen of standards-based reform.

Other scholars doubt that the two approaches mesh comfortably. In a paper prepared for the National Bureau of Economic Research, David Figlio and Marianne Page also looked at Florida. They contend that when vouchers are used as part of an accountability scheme keyed to school performance, youngsters who end up being aided are different from those who would be assisted by a more conventional voucher program focused on disadvantaged children.[7] This is because the distribution of low-income children in the state differs somewhat from the distribution of weak schools.

Despite their paper's provocative title ("Can School Choice and School Accountability Successfully Coexist?"), all Figlio and Page really accomplish is to make clear to policymakers that a single program probably cannot serve two separate policy goals equally well, and one must therefore either prioritize goals or else enact two separate policies. The authors, I believe, fail to show a fundamental conflict between Ted-style accountability and Alice's approach.

Still other scholars contend that Ted (standards) and Alice (markets) actually need each other in order to attain the maximum education reform and student achievement. In identifying five key components of an effective accountability system, for example, Kenneth Wong lists "pressure from market-like competition" alongside "setting standards," "formal sanctions,"

---

[6]Jay P. Greene, "An Evaluation of the Florida A-Plus Accountability and School Choice Program," Tallahassee: Florida State University, February 2001.

[7]David N. Figlio and Marianne E. Page, "Can School Choice and School Accountability Successfully Coexist?" working paper, National Bureau of Economic Research, January 2001.

"support to build up school capacity," and "support to build up student capacity."[8]

Herbert J. Walberg and Margaret C. Wang observe that these two forms of accountability actually have much in common and are "reconcilable" in both theory and practice. Both, they note, arise outside the traditional structures of public education governance and seek to put pressure on that system. Thus, "both reforms diminish traditional control in which local boards mediated among state boards, local taxpayers, parents, teachers, and other groups. . . ."[9] Both tend to concentrate money and control in individual schools while dividing power between those schools and external forces—and withdrawing it from the familiar public-education hierarchy. Instead of compliance with bureaucratic rules and procedures, both emphasize a school's results. Both, in other words, weaken Bob's control of the system. But they can easily live with one another.

The Ted (standards) and Alice (markets) pair is also at home with "tight-loose" management theory, which seems to underpin most successful modern ventures. In an organization run according to this theory, each production unit—in this case, an individual school—possesses wide authority to perform its work as it judges best but is held strictly accountable (by top executives, shareholders, etc.) for its "bottom line." Its results are closely monitored. Yet it doesn't have to produce them by following an elaborate manual of procedures. It is largely free to run itself. Thus, both accountability strategies overturn the ancient practice of public education (and most other government services), which is to regulate—Bob-style—via control of resources and processes rather than by each unit's success in producing the desired results through means of its own choosing.

---

[8]Kenneth K. Wong, "Integrated Government in Chicago and Birmingham (UK)," in *School Choice or Best Systems,* Margaret C. Wang and Herbert J. Walberg, editors, Mahwah, NJ: Lawrence Erlbaum Associates, 2001, p. 166.

[9]Wang and Walberg, op. cit., p. 375.

INTERDEPENDENCE

To my eye, the greatest source of interdependence between standards-based and market-style accountability is that each offers a promising solution to a big problem besetting the other. This may, in the end, prove to be the shotgun that causes Ted and Alice to wed, even though their kinfolk are none too cordial. Like partners in any successful marriage, each turns out to fare better when the other is around.

The first problem is that standards-based (i.e., Ted-style) accountability systems are better at identifying failing schools than at fixing them. Indeed, in most jurisdictions, the list of failing schools doesn't change much from one year to the next, despite all manner of technical assistance, professional development, extra resources, the importing of celebrated "whole school" models, and, of late, more aggressive efforts to reconstitute and outsource them. It would take another essay to examine *why* all these interventions seem to make so little difference. Suffice to say, bad schools are extremely hard to transform into good ones, particularly when the agents of their putative transformation are lumbering government bureaucracies working within a political environment where myriad interest groups (especially the schools' own employees and their organizations) have great power to block changes that they dislike. (Observe what happened when New York City education chancellor Harold O. Levy proposed to turn a few of his many failing schools over to Chris Whittle's Edison Schools for purposes of transformation.[10])

The upshot is that children enrolled in failing schools are apt to linger for many years in classrooms where they're learning very little. What's happened is that a pure Ted-style (standards-based) accountability system has succeeded in revealing shortcomings that it is incapable of fixing. That's obviously bad for the afflicted youngsters, but it also makes

[10]This saga is recounted in Edward Wyatt and Abby Goodnough, "As Bid to Privatize Schools Ends, Supporters Second Guess Effort," *New York Times,* March 31, 2001, and Abby Goodnough, "Scope of Loss for Privatizing By Edison Stuns Officials," *New York Times,* April 3, 2001.

a mockery of standards-based reform, which, in this scenario, is not actually accomplishing the reform of troubled schools. Ted illumines the problem, but he cannot solve it.

What to do? Ask Alice to lend a hand. Bring market forces to bear. Move the children to more effective schools, or turn them loose to move themselves. In other words, whether through assignment or volition, help them make their way from the failing schools to others that are succeeding. This is all but certain to benefit the youngsters who do move. And, as we have seen in Florida, Albany, Milwaukee, and elsewhere, it may also trigger needed changes in the schools they are leaving, which betters the lot of those youngsters who don't exit. Though the leaders of those schools will grouse—this is, after all, a painful therapy—the loss of students and revenue, combined with the possibility of closure, at least concentrates their minds on the problems they need to solve.

Both the charter school and voucher movements have begun to yield evidence that bad schools and school systems eventually respond to competition by trying to rectify the problems that led students (and revenues) to flee them. No, we don't yet have solid, large-scale data on the transformative effect of marketplace accountability. But we have suggestive research by Carolyn Hoxby indicating that school systems produce stronger results when they face competition, and we have lots of anecdotes, case studies, and small-scale research on charter schools that generally point in the same direction.[11]

---

[11]A series of papers by Professor Caroline Minter Hoxby that illuminate this subject can be found on her Web site at <http://post.economics.harvard.edu/faculty/hoxby/papers.html>. Particularly germane is her paper entitled "School Choice and School Productivity (or Could School Choice Be a Tide That Lifts All Boats?)," draft prepared for National Bureau of Economic Research conference, February 2001. This can be accessed on the Web at <http://post.economics.harvard.edu/faculty/hoxby/papers/school_choice.pdf>. Additionally, see Clive R. Belfield and Henry M. Levin, "The Effects of Competition on Educational Outcomes: A Review of US Evidence," Occasional Paper No. 35, National Center for the Study of Privatization in Education, Columbia University, September 2001. An abstract of this paper and a link to the PDF version can be found on the Web at <www.ncspe.org>.

This is all the more remarkable considering that most school-choice programs are as yet too small and new to have amounted to much more than a flea on the hide of an elephant in terms of their impact on the traditional school system.

More evidence is plainly needed. But there is reason to expect that the introduction of Alice-style competition into education will strengthen and vivify Ted-style accountability, even as it supplies salubrious educational alternatives for needy youngsters who might otherwise be stuck indefinitely in dysfunctional schools.

The converse is also true. Alice needs Ted. The education market is often flawed. Private schools, for example, frequently decline to take part in state tests because they don't want people making "simplistic" comparisons of their academic achievement. They prefer to rely on their reputations to market themselves to customers, perhaps burnishing their image as a "highly selective" school with "caring" teachers and solid college placements. Those attributes might all be true—but they might also be hype. Without a transparent marketplace based on uniform standards and rich with comparable and publicly accessible achievement data, one must trust every school to tell the truth. Thus, we could have a situation where schools are answerable to the marketplace, yet their consumers are unable to make informed choices among them. That leads in time to market failure. How can people know what school to choose—and resist false claims and unwarranted reputations—if they don't have the kinds of comparative performance data that are most apt to emerge from a system of uniform standards and tests? How will educators know which schools are most worth teaching in? How will prospective school founders know which education niches cry out to be filled with high-quality alternatives? How will policymakers know (for example) which charter schools deserve to have their contracts renewed? Absent data from a Ted-style, standards-based system, these various constituencies, stakeholders, and consumer groups may have nominal freedom to hold schools accountable via market forces, yet those markets will be inefficient and ill-informed.

If we're serious about accountability, therefore, we do well to consider the union of Ted and Alice. It appears—like most good marriages—to be an instance where the combination is stronger than the sum of its parts.

As for that antenuptial agreement, it's a good idea not because we must anticipate divorce but because it eases things by spelling out important assumptions that should accompany this marriage. Alice must, for example, agree to press for school and market transparency, using both Ted's data and information from individual schools, and she must agree that all schools need to be serious about producing results according to Ted's standards, as well as about satisfying their customers. Ted must agree to set sound standards in core subjects without trying to dictate every school's entire curriculum. He must align his assessments with his standards and ensure that they are accurately and swiftly scored. He must craft a "consequences" system that includes market forces such that, for example, children can leave bad schools for good schools of their choice. Both Alice and Ted should agree to be polite to Bob (compliance) but not let him take over their household. They should also agree to welcome visits from Carol (experts) but only when she's behaving sanely. (When she is, she can infuse knowledge, spirit, and focus into the educators responsible for satisfying both Ted's standards and Alice's clients.)

We could, of course, add many more provisions to this agreement. We know that neither Ted nor Alice is perfect. We believe that marriage will tend to bring out the best in both of them, however, and dampen the worst. Setting some ground rules will surely help. But let's face it: accountability in education is tough. Nobody has devised a powerful yet risk-free strategy. We will, therefore, be taking a risk with whatever approach we follow. So we must remain vigilant. But let's give this marriage a chance.

The Cost of Accountability

Caroline M. Hoxby

I. IS ACCOUNTABILITY EXPENSIVE?

A good accountability program includes a combination of testing, standards against which the test results can be compared, and report cards that relay this information (as well as information on schools' level and use of resources) to parents and policymakers. Proponents of school accountability tout the benefits of a well-run accountability system: information for teachers and principals who need to diagnose their students' progress, information that gives schools incentives to perform, information for parents who need to make choices among schools, and information on the degree to which schools are teaching the material that their constituents (parents, voters, school boards, legislators) want them to teach. In fact, school accountability programs are generally seen as *complementary* to other types of school reform. School choice, for instance, should work better if parents have more information, rather than less.

Opponents of school accountability mount arguments on two fronts: poor quality of tests and the expense of accountability. It is natural to care about the quality of tests because students will naturally spend time learning the material that is tested and schools will naturally tend to align their curricula with the material that is tested. Indeed, it is the *intention* of a good school accountability system that students study the material tested. The quality of tests and standards, though important, is the topic of other chapters in this book. This chapter focuses instead on the second argument against accountability—its expense. Some opponents of school accountability argue that it is so expensive that it will crowd out other policies, such as class size reduction or higher teacher salaries. Other opponents argue that it is so expensive to have a *good* accountability program (which includes good tests, well-defined standards, an effective report card system, and safeguards that prevent cheating) that only poor accountability systems will be affordable.

Understanding the cost of accountability turns out to be much simpler than understanding what makes a good test or set of standards. Facts are the best answer to questions about costs, so this chapter presents the facts. The facts about how much accountability costs, fortunately, are knowable. This is because the costs must show up in two places: as expenditure on some government's (usually the state's) budget and as revenue on some company's (mainly the test-maker's) accounts. A skeptic might ask, however: "Even if the accounting facts are knowable, won't they be imperfect? In one state, the salaries of state personnel who oversee the program might end up being counted as a cost of accountability; but another state might count such personnel as mere general staff of the state's department of education." This is a reasonable concern, but it turns out that such accounting details are not worthy of much worry. The costs of accountability programs are so small that even the most generous accounting could not make them appear large relative to the cost of other education programs.

II. WHAT TEST-MAKERS' REVENUES TELL US
ABOUT THE COST OF ACCOUNTABILITY

Nearly every achievement and ability test administered to American elementary and secondary school students is purchased from a commercial test-making firm, which also grades the test and prepares reports at the state, district, school, grade, class, and student levels. The same firms support their tests with curriculum guides, suggested standards for criterion-based tests, and materials designed to help schools understand the tests and standards and use them wisely. Indeed, test-makers tend also to be textbook publishers, so the knowledge on which they base tests and standards is generally the same knowledge that they must be able to defend for inclusion in textbooks.[1] The American elementary and secondary testing and standards industry is dominated by several well-known firms: Harcourt-Brace Educational Measurement, Reed-Elsevier, Houghton-Mifflin, Prentice-Hall, CTB/McGraw-Hill, and so on. In practice, these firms rely on similar psychometric research and routinely hire experts from one another. The firms publish tests with names that are nationally familiar (such as the Stanford 9, Comprehensive Test of Basic Skills/Terra Nova, and Iowa Test of Basic Skills), but they also write the states' specialized tests, such as the Connecticut Mastery Tests, the Texas Assessment of Academic Skills, Florida Writes, and *all* of the others.

Because of the small number and consistency of the firms involved, analysts have a very clear sense of the industry's revenue from accountability systems. According to the Association of American Publishers, the total revenue associated with accountability systems (revenue from sales of tests, revenue from standards-related materials such as curriculum guides and criteria, and revenue from services associated with

---

[1]The only important noncommercial elementary or secondary test is the National Assessment of Educational Progress, which is administered to a random sample of American students at the behest of the United States Department of Education.

accountability such as consulting for state government) amounted to $234.1 million in 2000. Because this figure includes a variety of intelligence quotient tests, diagnostic tests for disabled children, career guidance tests, and the like, it overstates firms' revenue associated with accountability. Nevertheless, the revenue amounts to only $4.96 per American student! Table 1 shows that even when we add in the cost of the National Assessment of Educational Progress, the only important elementary or secondary test *not* associated with a commercial test-maker, the cost of accountability is $5.81 per student. Such costs represent a very small share of the cost of educating American children: average per-pupil spending in the United States was $8,157 in the 2000–2001 school year. Put another way, payments to all test-makers (including the United States government) represented just 0.07 percent (seven-hundredths of 1 percent) of the cost of elementary and secondary education. Even if payments were *ten times as large,* they would still not be equal to 1 percent of what American jurisdictions spend on education.

In short, it seems likely that people who oppose accountability because of its costs have not investigated the revenue of test-makers, which suggest that the costs are extremely modest.

III. WHAT STATES' EXPENDITURES TELL US ABOUT THE COST OF ACCOUNTABILITY

Not all costs of state accountability systems end up as revenue that accrues to test-makers, however. States certainly can and do run accountability systems by just paying for tests, for publishing results, and for writing and publishing the standards on which the tests are graded. Indeed, such states spend *less* than $4.96 per student for their systems. Other states put more elaborate systems in place and have additional costs. For instance, some states have asked test-makers to design tests and curriculum guides that are specific to the state. Developing such materials costs more than using an "off-the-shelf" test, but the additional costs vary

TABLE 1

National Measures of the Cost of Assessment

	Total for United States (thousands)	Per Public School Pupil in United States
Standardized Testing Industry (Sales including tests, scoring, and distribution of score reports)	$234,100	$4.96
National Assessment of Educational Progress (cost of entire program; this national test is sample-based)	$40,000	$0.85

with the degree to which the state desires an idiosyncratic test. An assessment system that requires only modest adaptation and augmentation of a test-maker's existing materials will obviously cost less than an assessment system that has to be written nearly from scratch, albeit using much of the same knowledge and expertise that goes into off-the-shelf tests. Moreover, states can choose to create a larger or smaller bureaucracy associated with an accountability system. Whereas some states administer their systems with existing department of education staff or just a few additional staff, other states add numerous personnel who promulgate standards, run seminars for principals and teachers, and answer parents' questions. As a rule, states add more personnel when their accountability systems are more idiosyncratic (to the state) or more controversial with the public (so that more public relations are required). Also, a state that adds numerous personnel at the start-up of a system will often need fewer personnel to continue the system once the first few years are over and schools are accustomed to the process. Apart from payments to test-makers and their experts, a state's accountability budget may show some or all of the following expenses: the cost of running an office of accountability, the salaries of accountability bureaucrats at the state department of education, the cost of publishing school report cards (in addition to publishing test results and standards), the cost of ongoing redevelopment and evaluation of the system itself, the cost of consultants, and reimbursement to school districts for any costs that are imposed on them (such as training counselors on how to explain the system to parents). Because accountability systems tend to be popular with the public (according to Public Agenda, 94 percent of the public favor testing and standards), states have an incentive to exaggerate, not understate, the share of their department of education's overhead associated with accountability. Thus, once we add up a states' reported expenses for its accountability system (including payments to test-makers), we have (if anything) a slightly overstated sense of how much it costs a state to run a system.

Table 2 reviews the costs of twenty-five states' accountability systems. The twenty-five systems shown include the nation's most expensive systems because they naturally have the most specialized offices, which are the best at providing timely, detailed cost information. Table 2 shows which subjects are tested, which grades are tested, and both total and per-pupil costs. All of the states test reading (R) and mathematics (M), but some also test writing (W), science (S), social studies and history (SS), a foreign language (FL), the arts (A), vocational studies (V), computers and technology (C), or health and physical education (H). The most commonly tested grades are elementary and middle school grades, where off-the-shelf tests or modest adaptations of them are most appropriate. (There is widespread agreement that third graders ought to be numerate and able to read simple material. There is more controversy about what high school students should know.) Nevertheless, all but one of the twenty-five states test high school students—with a few testing students in every year of high school and several requiring a high school graduation test or high school competency exam.

TABLE 2
The Costs of Various States' Accountability Systems
(Fiscal Year 2001 Unless Otherwise Noted)

State	Subjects Tested*	Grades Tested**	State Total (000s)	Per Public School Pupil in State
California	R,W,M,S,SS,FL	2–12	$120,565	$19.93
Kentucky	R,W,M,S,SS,A,V	3–12	$11,662	$18.00
Texas	R,W,M,S,SS	3–12	$82,422	$20.30
Washington	R,W,M,S,SS	3–4,6–10	$14,910	$14.84
Virginia	R,W,M,S,SS,C	3–5,7–8,9–12	$19,251	$17.13
Arizona	R,W,M	1–9,12	$7,790	$8.72
Connecticut	R,W,M,S	4,6,8,10	$8,972	$16.20
Delaware	R,W,M,S,SS	3–6,8,10–11	$3,896	$34.02
Colorado	R,W,M,S	4–5,7–8,10	$11,769	$16.24
Georgia	R,W,M,S,SS	3–6,8,11	$6,809‡	$4.74
Idaho	R,W,M	2–9,11	$4,000	$16.32
Indiana	R,W,M,A	3,6,8,10	$24,284	$24.32
Minnesota	R,W,M	3,5	$11,289	$13.23
Michigan	R,M,S,SS	4,5,7,8,9–12	$16,400	$6.64
Ohio	R,W,M,S,SS	4,6,9,12	$15,692	$8.61
New Jersey	R,W,M,S	4,8,9–12	$16,688	$12.94
Pennsylvania	R,W,M	5,6,8,9,11	$15,000	$8.27
New Hampshire	R,W,M,S,SS	3,6,10	$2,100	$10.16
Massachusetts	R,W,M,S,SS	3–10	$19,169	$20.47
New York	R,W,M,S,SS	4,8,9–12	$13,314	$4.72
Wisconsin	R,W,M,S,SS	3,4,8,9–12	$5,240	$5.97
West Virginia	R,W,M	1–12	$3,622	$12.67
South Carolina	R,W,M	1,3–8,11	$1,196	$1.79
Maryland	R,W,M,S,SS	3,5,8,9–12	$20,540	$24.26
Missouri	R,W,M,S,SS,H	3–5,7–11	$13,730	$15.37

* The subjects listed are not necessarily tested in every grade listed. Both criterion-referenced and norm-referenced tests are listed. The abbreviations are: R=Reading (including a variety of English Language Arts, Spelling, and Listening tests), M=Mathematics, W=Writing, S=Science, SS=Social Studies and History (including advanced tests in global history, U.S. history, geography), FL=Foreign Language, A=Arts and Humanities, V=Vocational Studies, C=Computers and Technology, H=Health and Physical Education.

** The grades listed do not necessarily have tests administered in every subject listed.

‡ Data are for fiscal year 2002.

The per-pupil cost of accountability varies in Table 2, not only because states engage in different amounts of testing and have different "bells and whistles," but also because less-populated states spread the fixed costs of a system (especially an idiosyncratic system) over fewer pupils than large states do. At the low-cost end, there are states such as South Carolina ($1.79 per pupil) and Georgia ($4.74 per pupil). At the high-cost end, there are states such as Delaware ($34.02 per pupil) and Maryland ($24.26 per pupil). Even acknowledging that it is likely that states such as South Carolina understate the costs and that states such as Delaware overstate them, we have a good sense of the range. Just to keep things in perspective, note that even if every state had the per-pupil accountability costs that Delaware reports, their systems would still account for only 0.4 percent (less than one-half of 1 percent) of per-pupil expenditure on American public schools.

IV. CASE STUDIES SHOWING THE COSTS OF STATES' ACCOUNTABILITY SYSTEMS

While Table 2 gives us a good overall sense of the cost of accountability, curious readers may want to know more detail. I picked out several states with rather elaborate and well-documented accountability systems and investigated the details of their costs. Tables 3 through 8 show the results.

First, consider Arizona's system, the costs of which are presented in Table 3. Arizona is a fairly typical state in that it uses both an off-the-shelf test (the Stanford Achievement Test in grades 1 through 9) and a test designed specifically for the state (Arizona's Instrument to Measure Standards test, popularly known as "AIMS," in grades 3, 5, 8, and 12). Arizona tests students in reading, writing, and mathematics, a pattern that is also fairly typical. Arizona reports that the testing itself cost $5.93 per student, which is reasonable given the mix of inexpensive off-the-shelf tests and more expensive state-specific tests. Arizona has a student

TABLE 3
The Costs of Arizona's Accountability System (Fiscal Year 2001)

Activity Related to Arizona Assessment	Total for Arizona (thousands)	Per Public School Pupil in Arizona
Achievement Testing	$5,299	$5.93
Student Accountability Information System	2,003	2.24
School Report Card System	489	0.55
Total	$7,790	$8.72

Arizona's Instrument to Measure Standards Test: Reading (grades 3,5,8,12); Writing (grades 3,5,8,12); Mathematics (grades 4,7,10,12); Stanford Achievement Tests: Reading (grades 1–9), Mathematics (grades 1–9), Language (grades 1–9).

TABLE 4
The Costs of California's Accountability System (Fiscal Year 2001)

Activity Related to California Assessment	Total for California (thousands)	Per Public School Pupil in California
Public School Accountability Act Personnel	$1,905	$0.31
Public School Accountability Act Consultants	250	0.04
Test Experts for STAR and High School Exit Exam	360	0.06
New Personnel Required for STAR	400	0.07
Consultant for High School Exit Exam	107	0.02
Web site to Explain Assessment System	1,000	0.17
Activities to Ensure the Integrity of STAR and High School Exit Exam	210	0.03
Activities to Ensure that STAR and High School Exit Exam Are Aligned with California Standards	3,000	0.50

continued on next page

TABLE 4 (*continued*)

Reliability Testing of Golden State Exams	300	0.05
STAR Exam	65,643	10.85
High School Exit Exam	14,799	2.45
English Language Development Assessment	14,474	2.39
Test Development	12,000	1.98
Golden State Exam	1,493	0.25
Career Technical Assessment	843	0.14
Assessment Review and Reporting	3,781	0.62
Total	$120,565	$19.93

California Augmented Version of Stanford Test: Reading, Language, and Spelling (grades 2–11), Mathematics (grades 2–11), Science (grades 9–11), Social Studies (grades 9–11); High School Exit Exam; Golden State Exam: Reading/Language (grades 9–12), Written Composition (grades 9–12), Mathematics (grades 9–12), Science (grades 9–12), Spanish (grades 9–12), History and Social Science (grades 9–12).

TABLE 5
The Costs of Kentucky's Accountability System (Fiscal Year 2001)

Activity Related to Kentucky Commonwealth Accountability Testing System	Total for Kentucky (thousands)	Per Public School Pupil in Kentucky
Administration of System	$344	0.53
Implementation of System including:	10,736	16.57
Standards Setting		
Longitudinal Assessment		
Actual Administration of Test		
Portfolio Assessment		
School Report Cards		
Validation and Research Related to System	581	0.90
Total	$11,662	$18.00

Reading (grades 4,7,10), Mathematics (grades 5,9,11), Science (grades 4,7,11), Social Studies (grades 5,8,11), Arts and Humanities (grades 5,8,11), Writing (grades 4,7,12), Vocational Studies (grades 5,8,11), National Norm Referenced Test (grades 3,6,9).

TABLE 6
The Costs of Texas' Accountability System (Fiscal Year 2001)

Activity Related to Texas System	Total for Texas (thousands)	Per Public School Pupil in Texas
Governor's Reading Initiative	$25,000	$6.16
Texas Reading to Read Program	1,000	0.25
All Other Assessment Programs, Including Evaluation of Assessment System, Development of New Assessment Instruments, and Distribution of Study Guides	42,556	10.48
Successful Schools Award Program: Parent-Teacher Conference Component	500	0.12
Successful Schools Award Program: All Other Components	2,000	0.49
Accountability System Operations at Texas Education Agency, Including Computer and Software Consultants	11,366	2.80
Total	$82,422	$20.30

Reading (grades 3–8, high school exit), Mathematics (grades 3–8, high school exit), Science (grade 8), Social Studies (grade 8), Writing (grades 4,8, high school exit), Algebra (end of course), Biology (end of course), U.S. History (end of course), English II (end of course), Reading Proficiency in English (limited English students, grades 3–12), State Developed Alternative Assessment (special education students).

accountability information system that follows each student's progress over time, computes value-added for each student, and tracks each student's grade progression and movement among schools. The information system is run through an office of the state department of education and costs $2.24 per pupil. Finally, Arizona publishes the test results, its standards, and a myriad of other information about schools (staffing, enrollment, mission, special programs, spending) in a school report card. These report cards are not only distributed to parents and policymakers;

TABLE 7
The Costs of Washington's Accountability System
(Fiscal Year 2002)

Activity Related to Washington Assessment of Student Learning	Total for Washington (thousands)	Per Public School Pupil in Washington
Assessment Implementation	$11,209	$11.16
Continuing Development of Assessment	3,000	2.99
Assessment "Institutes" that Teach School Staff to Interpret Results	500	0.50
Interpretation Training for Second-Grade Teachers	71	0.07
Internet Posting of Assessment Results	130	0.13
Total	$14,910	$14.84

Washington Tests: Reading (grades 4,7,10), Mathematics (grades 4,7,10), Writing (grades 4,7,10), Listening (grades 4,7,10), Science (grades 8,10), Iowa Test of Basic Skills (grades 3,6), Iowa Test of Educational Development (grade 9).

TABLE 8
The Costs of Virginia's Accountability System
(Fiscal Year 2001)

Activity Related to Virginia Standards of Learning System	Total for Virginia (thousands)	Per Public School Pupil in Virginia
Development and Administration of Materials and Tests Related to Standards of Learning	$17,968	$15.99
Literacy Passport Test	923	0.82
Pilots of Online Testing, Electronic Materials	360	0.32
Total	$19,251	$17.13

Virginia Standards of Learning Tests: Writing (grades 3,5,8), Mathematics (grades 4,7,10), English and Reading (grades 3,5,8), Science (grades 3,5,8), History and Social Studies (grades 3,5,8), Computers and Technology (grades 3,5,8), World History (grades 9–12), U.S. History (grades 9–12), World Geography (grades 9–12).

they are also made available at all public libraries and can be viewed on (and downloaded from) a dedicated Web site. The report card system costs $0.55 per pupil so that Arizona's system costs a total of $8.72 per pupil. Arizona's system is widely perceived as a system that is comprehensive without being overbearing (Arizona does not use it to enforce a particular curriculum), and part of the fame of the state superintendent who implemented it, Lisa Graham Keegan, is due to the system's being a model for other states. Thus, it is reasonable to take Arizona's $8.72 per pupil as a benchmark for a comprehensive but not-over-elaborate system.

California has a system that is considerably more elaborate, especially at present. This is because California is in the midst of modifying one system (STAR) and designing another (the Golden State Exams), so it is simultaneously paying for the development of multiple tests. California has a specially adapted and augmented version of the Stanford Achievement Test (STAR), which it uses in grades 2 through 11 to test reading, language, spelling, mathematics, science (grades 9 through 11 only), and social studies (grades 9 through 11 only). California is also paying for a high school exit exam and the state-specific Golden State Exams, which are tests for grades 9 through 12 in reading, language, written composition, mathematics, science, Spanish, and history and social science. California also has an array of activities that complement its exams: seminars for school staff, experts to explain the system, experts to evaluate how the system is aligned with California's standards, ongoing evaluation and review of the system, and a few additional tests (English language development and career assessment). In short, California's system is elaborate not only because it is very comprehensive; it is elaborate also because California is fully in the midst of its development. One might think that such a system would be expensive, but the total cost per pupil is $19.93, about twice that of Arizona's system but still a very small 0.2 percent (two-tenths of 1 percent) of American per-pupil spending.

Personnel to administer California's system include new department of education staff for the Public School Accountability Act ($0.31 per pupil) and STAR tests ($0.07 per pupil), consultants for the Public School Accountability Act ($0.04 per pupil) and high school exit exam ($0.02 per pupil), and test experts for STAR and the high school exit exam ($0.06 per pupil). These personnel may seem like a lot, but when spread over all the students in a state, their salaries and fees just do not amount to much ($0.50 per pupil). Similarly, the total cost of complementary activities is a modest $3.60 per pupil. The complementary activities include a Web site ($0.17 per pupil); test integrity ($0.03 per pupil); alignment with state standards ($0.50 per pupil); reliability testing ($0.05 per pupil); test development, including that of the Golden State Exams ($1.98 + $0.25 per pupil); and assessment review ($0.62 per pupil). In short, in California it is still the tests themselves that generate the bulk of the costs, and we have already seen that these costs are not great.

Kentucky has a well-known assessment system, partly because its system has some unusual elements such as longitudinal assessment (a complex value-added system in which expert statisticians control for student characteristics) and portfolio assessment, in which students' actual classroom work is assembled in a structured portfolio and analyzed by an outside expert, such as an educator. In other words, Kentucky's system contains a high degree of individuation for each student and has features that require many hours of work from expert consultants. Kentucky is, thus, a useful benchmark for anyone interested in individuated systems. The state's Commonwealth Accountability Tests are administered in grades 4, 5, 7, 8, 9, 10, 11, and 12, although not every subject is administered in every grade. The subjects are diverse: reading, mathematics, science, social studies, arts and humanities, writing, and vocational studies. Kentucky also administers an off-the-shelf norm-referenced test in grades 3, 6, and 9, partly to ensure that the state-specific tests remain comparable to other American tests.

Although Kentucky's expenditure statements do not contain as much detail as we would like, they do inform us that implementing the system (including setting the standards, administering the test, assessing the portfolios, performing longitudinal assessment, and distributing school report cards) costs a total of $16.57 per student. This is almost twice as much as Arizona's system, but the longitudinal and portfolio assessment *are* more expensive evaluation methods. The Kentucky Commonwealth Accountability Testing System also requires $0.53 per pupil for administration and $0.90 per pupil for ongoing validation and research related to the system.

The Texas system of assessment and accountability is one of the most comprehensive in the United States. The state administers the Texas Assessment of Academic Skills test in reading and math in grades 3 through 8 and at the high school exit level. Texas also tests social studies and science in grade 8, and it tests writing in grades 4 and 8 and at the high school exit level. There are end-of-course examinations in algebra, biology, U.S. history, and English II. Tests are administered in both English and Spanish, and they are fully integrated with Texas' standards for every grade (the Texas Essential Knowledge and Skills). Students with limited En-glish proficiency take the Reading Proficiency Test in English in grades 3 through 12, and special education students take the State-Developed Alternative Assessment. The state is currently spending money on the development of tests for gifted and talented students. The Texas Education Agency has what is almost certainly the most developed database system in the United States for tracking student achievement. Indeed, every student is followed as an individual (longitudinally), regardless of where he or she moves in the state. Students are even being followed into the college system. Texas makes many of its data and reports available online, both in user-friendly forms for parents and in databases for researchers. Schools are evaluated, and school report cards are distributed and publicized. Schools receive modest rewards for good performance.

Texas' comprehensive system costs $20.30 per student. This includes the rewards for schools, continuing development and evaluation of the program, and maintaining the data systems that track students. Of this total, $6.41 is spent on the two reading assessment programs for young students, and $10.48 is spent on all the other tests. The reward program spends $0.49 per student rewarding schools for doing well on the assessment instruments and spends another $0.12 per student rewarding schools that get a high percentage of parents to attend parent-teacher conferences. Assessment costs $0.61 per student. Administration, computers, and consultants account for the remaining $2.80 per student.

Finally, let us consider the states of Washington and Virginia, which differ from Arizona's typical system mainly because the two states have *just* begun to implement state-specific tests. In other words, Washington and Virginia are at the most expensive stage that a state can expect to experience when setting up a state-specific system. In the first few years, implementing an assessment system is not routine, so it costs more. Also, in its first few years, a system continues to be developed and needs to be explained to educators and the public.

Washington State administers state-specific tests in reading, mathematics, writing, listening, and science. These tests focus on grades 4, 7, and 10. The state also administers the Iowa Test of Basic Skills in grades 3 and 6 and administers the Iowa Test of Educational Development in grade 9. Implementing this new system cost $11.16 per student. Continuing development of the system costs an additional $2.99 per student, and outreach efforts to explain the system to educators and parents cost $0.70 per student. The total is $14.84 per student.

Virginia has developed an ambitious set of state-specific tests called Virginia Standards of Learning. The tests are given mainly in grades 3, 5, and 8 and in high school. Several subjects are tested: writing, mathematics, English and reading, science, social studies, computers and technology, world history, U.S. history, and world geography. The implementation and continuing development of these tests cost $15.99 per student. In addition, Virginia administers a literacy test ($0.82 per student) and is working on an online version of its test and related curricular materials ($0.32 per student). The total is $17.13 per student.

V. PUTTING ASSESSMENT COSTS IN PERSPECTIVE

People who argue against accountability systems based on their costs often claim that the systems will crowd out other school programs. Recalling this argument, it is useful to put the costs of accountability in perspective by considering (1) per-pupil spending in the United States and (2) the costs of two popular policies, class size reduction and higher teacher salaries. Table 9 shows the statistics for all fifty states and for the United States as a whole.

Examine the top row of Table 9, which shows the United States as a whole. In 2000–01, per-pupil spending was $8,157 on average. A reduction in class size requires a proportional increase in the number of teachers and a proportional increase in school building size that is one-for-one with the proportional reduction in class size. For instance, 10 percent more teachers and 10 percent more classrooms are needed if class size is to be reduced by 10 percent. A 10 percent reduction in class size translates in two fewer students per class in most of America, so a 10 percent reduction is not negligible, yet it is unlikely to change the nature of teaching. (Reducing class size to, say, ten students per class would be more likely to change the nature of teaching, but it would also represent a 50 percent reduction in class size—five times more costly than the policy shown in Table 9!) Given that teacher compensation represents 54 percent of the average American school's cost and that items proportional to the size of school buildings (building, heating, etc.) represent another 22 percent of the average American school's cost, a 10 percent reduction in class size costs about $615 per student in

TABLE 9
Putting Accountability Costs in Perspective: School Spending in the United States

State	Per-Pupil Spending* (2000–2001)	% of Spending that Is Teacher Compensation	% of Spending that Is Proportional to School Building Size	Approximate Per-Pupil Cost of Reducing Class Size by 10%	Approximate Per-Pupil Cost of Raising Teacher Compensation by 10%
United States	$8,157	54	22	$615	$437
Alabama	6,921	53	20	509	370
Alaska	10,098	52	22	740	521
Arizona	6,531	45	31	495	295
Arkansas	5,927	58	18	448	341
California	7,466	54	21	557	400
Colorado	6,775	48	25	496	325
Connecticut	11,209	57	18	844	644
Delaware	9,725	57	17	719	552
District of Columbia	11,540	40	23	721	458

Florida	$7,913	50	25	$589	$394
Georgia	8,219	54	20	610	443
Hawaii	7,424	56	20	567	416
Idaho	7,003	53	23	532	372
Illinois	7,938	51	25	600	405
Indiana	8,622	52	26	671	447
Iowa	7,581	55	19	555	414
Kansas	7,749	52	19	553	404
Kentucky	7,280	57	15	524	418
Louisiana	6,672	54	17	477	363
Maine	8,884	62	16	697	554
Maryland	8,938	56	19	670	504
Massachusetts	9,998	64	13	765	639
Michigan	9,236	50	24	684	458
Minnesota	8,478	52	24	645	443
Mississippi	5,639	52	23	422	295
Missouri	7,489	54	21	559	403
Montana	7,250	57	19	546	411
Nebraska	8,393	56	19	629	467

continued on next page

TABLE 9 (continued)

State	Per-Pupil Spending* (2000–01)	% of Spending that is Teacher Compensation	% of Spending that is Proportional to School Building Size	Approximate Per-Pupil Cost of Reducing Class Size by 10%	Approximate Per-Pupil Cost of Raising Teacher Compensation by 10%
Nevada	$6,829	47	30	$524	$319
New Hampshire	7,949	59	17	605	471
New Jersey	12,199	55	19	896	669
New Mexico	7,084	49	24	512	344
New York	10,950	60	20	874	653
North Carolina	7,073	52	24	536	369
North Dakota	7,746	55	18	564	429
Ohio	8,621	53	19	619	455
Oklahoma	6,381	54	19	464	344
Oregon	7,774	53	20	570	411
Pennsylvania	9,549	54	24	741	517
Rhode Island	9,299	65	11	707	602
South Carolina	7,622	49	24	563	377

South Dakota	$7,042	52	24	$536	$364
Tennessee	6,217	57	20	481	357
Texas	7,057	51	26	545	359
Utah	5,654	54	26	451	306
Vermont	9,769	59	17	737	574
Virginia	8,109	53	21	604	433
Washington	7,882	49	25	583	384
West Virginia	7,892	56	19	590	442
Wisconsin	9,266	54	23	709	498
Wyoming	8,710	52	24	666	454

* Total public school spending divided by total public school membership, 2000–01 United States Department of Education estimates.

the United States. Put another way, a modest reduction in class size costs 7,053 percent more than an accountability system like Arizona's and 12,399 percent more than the current average cost of assessment (see Table 1). Given that a modest class size reduction is about three *orders of magnitude* more expensive than an accountability system, the claim that significant crowd-out occurs is simply unfactual. If a state were in the midst of reducing class size, implementing an accountability system like Arizona's (without increasing the budget) would turn a 10 percent class size reduction to a 9.9 percent class size reduction. No one would notice the difference between these two class size reduction policies! The lower rows of Table 9 show the cost of reducing class size by 10 percent for all fifty states. The amount varies around the national average of $615, from $422 per student in Mississippi to $896 per student in New Jersey.

Now consider a 10 percent increase in teacher compensation. Although teachers would undoubtedly be grateful for such a raise and view it as useful, such a raise would not dramatically change the skill level of people who enter and remain in teaching. Thus, a 10 percent increase in compensation could be described as significant but not transforming. Table 9 shows that it would cost the average American school $437 per student to raise teachers' compensation by 10 percent. (The low is $295 per student in Mississippi and the high is $669 in New Jersey.) In other words, raising teacher salaries by 10 percent costs 5,011 percent more than an accountability system like Arizona's and 8,810 percent more than the current average cost of assessment (see Table 1). Again, a claim of crowd-out bears little relationship to the facts. If a state were in the midst of raising teacher compensation, implementing an accountability system like Arizona's (without increasing the budget) would turn a 10 percent raise for teachers into a 9.8 percent raise. If a 9.8 percent raise were not going to change teachers, a 10 percent raise would not do so, either!

Table 10, the final table in this chapter, puts accountability costs into perspective using per-pupil spending. The table shows the *actual* share of per-pupil spending that is devoted to various states' accountability systems. It also shows the *actual* share for the United States as a whole. The nation spends 0.06 percent (six-hundredths of 1 percent) of funds for elementary and secondary public schools on assessment. Although the states on the table include those with elaborate accountability programs, no state spends *even 1 percent* of its elementary and secondary school budget on accountability. The top spenders' actual spending is about one-third of 1 percent of their public school budgets. In short, assessment accounts for a tiny, almost negligible portion of American school costs at present. People who oppose accountability based on its great cost ought to examine publicly available budget statements.

VI. OUGHT ACCOUNTABILITY SYSTEMS BE MORE EXPENSIVE, PREVENTING CHEATING?

One of the most frequent complaints about accountability systems is that schools "teach to the test." This criticism generally confuses two complaints, one of which is legitimate and the other of which is wrong-headed. The wrong-headed complaint is that schools "teach *toward* the test." A school that teaches *toward* a test modifies its curriculum in order to present material that will help students answer the types of questions that appear on the assessment tests. This complaint is misguided because the *intention* of assessment is to induce schools to alter their practices (if necessary) so that their students acquire the knowledge the state thinks they ought to know. Though we may worry that states make imperfect decisions about what students ought to know, such worries are best addressed by improving the assessment instruments, not by relieving schools of the responsibility to demonstrate that they generate knowledge.

TABLE 10
Putting Accountability Costs in Perspective:
Accountability Costs as a Share of Public School Spending

State	Cost of Assessment Per Pupil*	Per-Pupil Spending (2000–2001)	Cost of Assessment as a Percentage of Per-Pupil Spending
United States	$4.96	$8,157	0.06
Arizona	8.72	6,531	0.01
California	19.93	7,466	0.27
Colorado	16.24	6,775	0.24
Connecticut	16.20	11,209	0.14
Delaware	34.02	9,725	0.35
Georgia	4.74	8,219	0.06
Idaho	16.32	7,003	0.23
Indiana	24.32	8,622	0.28
Kentucky	18.00	7,280	0.25
Maryland	24.26	8,938	0.27
Massachusetts	20.47	9,998	0.20
Michigan	6.64	9,236	0.07
Minnesota	13.23	8,478	0.16
Missouri	15.37	7,489	0.21
New Hampshire	10.16	7,949	0.13
New Jersey	12.94	12,199	0.11
New York	4.72	10,950	0.04
Ohio	8.61	8,621	0.10
Pennsylvania	8.27	9,549	0.09
South Carolina	1.79	7,622	0.02
Texas	20.30	7,057	0.29
Virginia	17.13	8,109	0.21
Washington	14.84	7,882	0.19
West Virginia	12.67	7,892	0.16
Wisconsin	5.97	9,266	0.06

* Cost of assessment per pupil are from Table 2.

The legitimate complaint is that schools may "teach *the test*"—that is, give students specific answers to specific questions that appear on the test. Schools may do this through outright cheating (writing answers on the board, filling in students' answer sheets for them, looking at the actual test ahead of time and making students memorize sequences of answers). Schools may also do this by giving teachers access to the tests before and after the actual administration of the test so that teachers incorporate actual questions and answers from the test into their course materials. Using such methods, a school could improve scores without its students acquiring the base of knowledge for which the test questions were written.

Fortunately, it turns out that a bit of money can solve the legitimate concern about *teaching the test*. Elementary and secondary schools could use outside proctors to deliver the tests just before test time, administer and proctor the tests, and collect the tests and return them to the test-maker (who scores them). With proctors, teachers would not be in contact with the tests at all and would have to rely on the state's curricular guidance to align their students' knowledge with the tests (this is exactly what the state wants them to do). Outside proctors would cost between $1 and $4 per student, depending on the number of grades and subjects that a state decides to test. The maximum predicted cost of $4 per student is a bit under 0.05 percent (five-hundredths of 1 percent) of American per-pupil spending. We could go beyond proctors and insist that tests be based on larger batteries of questions (so that even students' recollections could not be used to predict the questions on next year's test). Test-makers typically raise the cost of a test by about 10 percent if they are asked to supply fresh questions each year. Freshness in and of itself does not cost much because test-makers can easily write numerous versions of a specific type of question. Greater freshness is not the same as test *development,* in which a type of question is written and validated "from scratch." In short, given that the average amount spent on tests now is $4.96 per student, fresh tests would cost about $5.46 per student if schools were generally to ask for them (still about six-tenths of 1 percent of American school spending). However, with good proctors, fresh test questions are not as necessary.

VII. FINAL THOUGHTS ON THE COST OF ACCOUNTABILITY SYSTEMS

Every statistic contained in this chapter is taken from sources that are publicly, readily available. Thus, people who oppose accountability based on its costs have probably neglected to do their homework and collect the facts. Assessment systems are very inexpensive by any metric, even when we consider elaborate and still-in-development systems such as California's.

What conclusions ought we to draw from the fact that accountability systems are so inexpensive? First, given the systems' low costs, we ought not to hesitate to improve them (by adding proctors, developing better tests, and so on) if the improvements would generate better incentives for schools. The cost of such improvements can come from other programs that will be only negligibly affected because they are so much more expensive. Second, accountability is so cheap, compared to other programs that are popular and under debate (such as class size reduction), that assessment should be given the benefit of the doubt. Even if the benefits of accountability are small, its benefit-to-cost ratio is likely to be extremely high relative to that of other programs. Thus, even when a state's budget prevents it from pursuing many of the programs that parents and policymakers would like to see enacted, the state should still try putting some assessment in place. Having assessment in place will also make it easier to evaluate the effects of other reforms. Finally, it is well known that the federal government accounts for only a small share (between 6 and 7 percent, depending on the year) of the revenue of American elementary and secondary schools. It is often difficult for the federal government to find programs that are both potentially important and affordable within its small education budget. The federal government could very plausibly pay for a basic level of assessment in every state, thereby encouraging all states to craft accountability systems that suit them but still meet minimal guidelines (for instance: testing at least reading and mathematics; testing at least one elementary, one middle, and one high school grade; using a national test in some grade to facilitate comparisons among states).

The costs of accountability are such that the main barrier to good programs is not expense but the support and interest of education experts, policymakers, and the public. Given the popularity of accountability with the public, educators and policymakers are the key people who will enable or disable a state attempting to implement a useful accountability system.

Sorting Out Accountability Systems

Eric A. Hanushek and Margaret E. Raymond

Accountability has been a catchword in education for decades, for who could be against it? It has not been a reality, however, because accountability threatens many and because, even when desired, it is difficult to implement. There are signs, however, that times are changing. Today, accountability is not only taken more seriously but also sometimes promises to have real teeth. Yet the future is far from certain. Although many states and districts are moving forward with accountability schemes, they are likely to run into real problems that compromise and distort these programs' impact. Though it seems natural to measure outcomes and hold schools responsible for them, the mechanics of how to do that appropriately are complicated. Creating effective accountability schemes will require a deeper understanding of how these programs alter incentives in schools and in turn the dynamics of accountability.[1] Understanding these issues is important because many people tend to generalize erroneously from problems imbedded in specific accountability systems to assertions of inherent weaknesses in all accountability systems.

---

[1] These considerations are also not unique to schools. The recent growth of research into corporate accountability systems underscores how the simplicity of the idea contrasts with the reality of the application.

Considerable controversy accompanies accountability in schools. Parents, teachers, policymakers, and the American public frequently enter into debate about various elements and uses of accountability systems. These debates are motivated by different underlying views about how best to improve the education of our youth as well as by self-interested reactions. This discussion does not dwell on the controversies but instead focuses on the key elements that enter into the incentives that are created by them.

The origin of today's need for accountability can be traced to the historical development of the U.S. educational system, which is thus briefly reviewed here. The structure and function of current accountability systems are then described. Following that, issues brought up by implementation and program impacts are discussed.

The importance of the accountability movement should not, however, be missed. By focusing attention on student performance, the policy debate has dramatically shifted. The challenge now is capitalizing on this movement to bring about improvements in outcomes.

THE STATE OF U.S. EDUCATION

Understanding the dynamics of the U.S. educational system sheds light on the current thrust toward accountability and the issues facing today's policymakers. In simplest terms, student performance has stagnated while costs have steadily increased. These simple facts have led to the realization that just providing more resources within the current structure is unlikely to be effective. Nor does adding further regulation offer much promise.

This stagnation is illustrated by the results of the National Assessment of Educational Progress (NAEP), which annually tests students across the country in different subject areas. The tests, which have been conducted over the past three decades, start with a random sample of students from different grade levels. A summary of the performance of 17-year-olds over time is provided in Figure 1. This figure tracks average scores

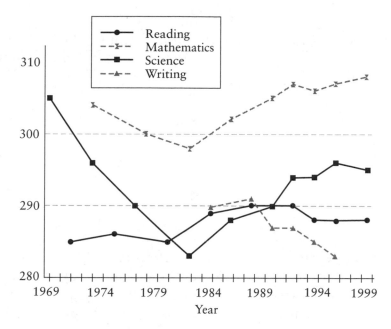

FIGURE 1. National Assessment of Educational
Progress—17-year-olds

in reading, math, science, and writing.[2] The story is one of flat achievement. Reading and math scores are slightly higher at the end of three decades, whereas science and writing appear to have noticeably declined.

Level performance would not be a matter of serious concern except for two important additional trends. First, it parallels mediocre performance on the international level, where the United States has performed at or below average since the 1960s.[3] Second, the lackluster U.S. performance has not been for want of trying. As Table 1 shows, school resources have been increased over the same period of time. Real spending per

---

[2] The writing tests were first introduced in 1986 and then dropped after 1996 because of concerns about both the expense and the reliability of the tests over time.

[3] At least in recent years, these results do not reflect international differences in selectivity of schooling or test taking but instead appear to reflect more fundamental forces. A summary of the performance of countries across the tests along with references to the basic data can be found in Eric A. Hanushek and Dennis D. Kimko, "Schooling, Labor Force Quality, and the Growth of Nations," *American Economic Review* 90, no. 5 (2000): 1184–1208.

TABLE 1
Public School Resources in the United States, 1960–1995

Resource	1960	1970	1980	1990	1995
Pupil-teacher ratio	25.8	22.3	18.7	17.2	17.3
% teachers with master's degree or more	23.5	27.5	49.6	53.1	56.2
Median years teacher experience	11	8	12	15	15
Current expenditure/ADA (1996–97 $s)	$2,122	$3,645	$4,589	$6,239	$6,434

student more than tripled between 1960 and 1995.[4] This increase in resources was accomplished in the way typically called for by reformers and policymakers: by significantly reducing pupil-teacher ratios, by increasing the training of teachers, and by developing a more experienced teaching force.

The dominant approach to policymaking over much of this period has been regulation of education inputs and processes. Efforts have been concentrated on providing resources for specific programs in the schools. This approach has been especially appealing to legislatures and courts—the places where overall fiscal decisions tend to be made—because it is easy to set resource policy. But, as shown in the aggregate data, increased resources have not improved performance. Moreover, these overall impressions have

---

[4]Some have argued that the simple data on resources overstate what is available for schools for improvement. Specifically, because of productivity increases in other industries, wages of educated workers in schools (teachers) are driven up, and the price deflators for school spending might be too low (Richard Rothstein and Karen Hawley Miles, *Where's the Money Gone? Changes in the Level and Composition of Education Spending*, Washington, DC: Economic Policy Institute, 1995). Additionally, increased demands such as those generated by laws for special education may draw resources away from the regular education students who are tested by NAEP. Each of these arguments has some legitimacy but cannot eliminate the significant rise in real resources devoted to schools (see Eric A. Hanushek and Steven G. Rivkin, "Understanding the Twentieth-Century Growth in U.S. School Spending," *Journal of Human Resources* 32, no. 1 (1997): 35–68).

been reinforced by similar findings of analyses of performance across classrooms and schools.[5] And there is little evidence that the special emphasis of the courts on the distribution of outcomes (expressed, however, in terms of required changes in funding distributions) has narrowed variation in student results.[6]

This lack of improved performance has brought attention to alternative means of effecting change in schools. This attention has been manifested in a variety of forms (discussed below), but a common theme has been the regulation of outcomes rather than the more traditional regulation of process and inputs. Previous efforts were based on providing or prescribing specific inputs (such as reduced class size in specific circumstances) and hoping that these led to improved student performance. Often, however, these decisions were based on little information that would indicate high probabilities of success. The new regulatory frameworks tend to emphasize objective outcomes while letting schools decide how they would meet demands for achievement. The underlying idea is that public monitoring and reporting of student outcomes would drive innovation and competition in schools and would bring about improvement.

A prime example of the change to performance focus is the development of Goals 2000. Because of concerns about school performance, the nation's governors met in an unprecedented summit with President George H.W. Bush in 1989. As a result of this meeting, a commitment was made to a set of national educational goals. These goals included such resolutions as "the United States should be first in the

---

[5]Eric A. Hanushek, "Assessing the Effects of School Resources on Student Performance: An Update," *Educational Evaluation and Policy Analysis* 19, no. 2 (1997): 141–164.

[6]Thomas A. Downes, "Evaluating the Impact of School Finance Reform on the Provision of Public Education: The California Case," *National Tax Journal* 45, no. 4 (1992): 405–419; Eric A. Hanushek and Julie A. Somers, "Schooling, Inequality, and the Impact of Government," in *The Causes and Consequences of Increasing Inequality*, Finis Welch, editor, Chicago: University of Chicago Press, 2001.

world in science and math performance by 2000." Though
this bit of wishful thinking later was belied by international
test scores, it nonetheless underscored the movement toward
measurable goals based on student outcomes.[7]

The Goals 2000 ideas blended into what is today perhaps
the most acclaimed path to educational improvement: the
so-called "standards-based reform." This approach to education reform relies on setting educational goals and measuring progress toward them. Public disclosure of both is
considered a feasible way to ensure goal achievement.
Nonetheless, there are many ways to implement this approach, suggesting that achieving the results desired is not
automatic.

For the present discussion, it is sufficient to note that attention to results created by these reform efforts has moved
most states to begin development of accountability systems.
The design, use, and impact of such systems is the subject of
this analysis.

The underlying perspective throughout this analysis is that
accountability systems should be viewed as an inherent
source of incentives designed to push schools toward desired
outcomes. The ultimate impact of accountability efforts depends upon the precision and force of the incentives they
create.

SEA CHANGE IN POLICY PERSPECTIVE

Accountability systems have been developed almost universally across the states to deal with the aggregate performance
shortcomings that are now widely recognized. That history
has shown that we do not know how to link programs,
resources, and other inputs to student outcomes so that

---

[7]Subsequent modifications of the original goals have added confusion, however,
by moving more toward inputs as opposed to outcomes. Instead of considering just
school completion, performance, and so forth, the goals now include expanding
parental participation in education and ensuring safe and drug-free schools.

regulation of inputs cannot be assumed to satisfy outcome objectives. The sea change of moving from a basic regulatory environment to one that emphasizes performance and outcomes can be interpreted as recognition that something else has to be done.

The importance of this changed perspective should not be underestimated. *If one is interested in outcomes, one should focus on outcomes.* As simple as this principle might be, it has not been recognized previously.

States now routinely develop snapshots of how students are doing in each year. To varying extents, they also use these snapshots to provide views about the performance of schools and teachers.

These systems are premised on an assumption that a focus on student outcomes will lead to behavioral changes by students, teachers, and schools to align with the performance goals of the system. Part of this is presumed to be more or less automatic (i.e., a public reporting of outcomes will bring everybody onto course to improve those outcomes). But part also comes from the development of explicit incentives that will lead to innovation, efficiency, and fixes to any observed performance problems.

The governance of schools is, nonetheless, currently in transition. States have not entirely bought into an exclusive focus on outcomes. They are reluctant to let go completely of a long tradition of input regulation. A benign interpretation is that tracking inputs and processes can provide important comparative data to understand better the distribution of outcomes. However, a more prescriptive treatment of inputs, though conflicting with the overall intent and working of accountability for outcomes, may also reflect a combination of uncertainty about how to design an outcome-based system along with political pressures to do other things.

Our question is simply, Given what states are doing, is it likely that we will get to the improved performance that is desired and expected?

CURRENT PRACTICE[8]

The basic skeleton of accountability systems involves goals, content standards, measurement, consequences, and reporting. Although states differ in significant ways, a general description of the structure of these systems is useful in comparing actual plans and how their elements interact. Below is a description of each element, followed by a look at currently unanswered questions.

Goals.   An accountability system begins with a set of goals about what is to be accomplished by the accountability system. Though this is often phrased in very general and lofty terms (e.g., "ensure that all students have sufficient skills to participate in society"), the goals have a distinct role because precise standards and measurements are usually based on these goals. Nonetheless, most states' goals are created in the underlying statutes that create their accounting systems, leaving them frequently ambiguous and difficult to measure. Though perhaps necessary to ensure legislative approval, such vaguely worded goals leave real ambiguity about what is to be done by whom.

A notable aspect of the goals statements of accountability systems that can have real impact is where they place the focus of attention—that is, whether they focus on students, schools, or teachers. In the current development, it is frequently suggested that each group feels targeted, although the degree of attention to each differs significantly across states. The differences in focus are often related to the strength of incentives ultimately generated for each participant in the system.

Content Standards.   Content standards typically present the details of what is expected. They create boundaries or domains for attention. The typical student outcome standards

---

[8]The profiles of current accountability system practices are based on data from "Quality Counts 2001: A Better Balance," *Education Week,* January 11, 2001.

delineate to what extent students should demonstrate mastery of a body of material that has been designated by an authoritative body to represent a minimum acceptable set of knowledge. Forty-nine states have established academic standards for student achievement: thirty-six states have standards in English or language arts, forty-four in mathematics, forty-three in science, and twenty-seven in social studies. Many researchers believe that this movement to explicit measurement of performance is key to current school reforms.[9]

Standards involve selection of a subset of all possible elements in a domain to both represent the whole and to be used to extrapolate more generalized performance. Although apparently straightforward, the creation of precise standards has been fraught with difficulty. Tension exists between the need for a representative set of elements and the need for the elements to be testable (discussed below). Tensions also exist between standards and learning goals; take the opposition, for example, between those who advocate rigorous standards and those who say such standards do not adequately assess higher-order curriculum or reasoning.

Standards are introduced in order to change behavior. The current standards-based reform explicitly argues that the development of standards will (almost necessarily) lead to better performance. As a snapshot of the interim effect of adopting standards, a national survey asked teachers if they had altered their classroom behavior.[10] The majority of respondents indicated that standards have necessitated more challenging curriculum and a focus on material delineated by the standards. This internal view has, however, yet to be matched with evidence that student performance has been

---

[9]Cf. Richard F. Elmore, Charles H. Abelmann, and Susan H. Fuhrman, "The New Accountability in State Education Reform: From Process to Performance," in *Holding Schools Accountable: Performance-Based Reform in Education*, Helen F. Ladd, editor, Washington, DC: Brookings Institute Press, 1996: 65–98.

[10]Belden, Russonello, and Stewart, *Making the Grade: Teachers' Attitudes toward Academic Standards and State Testing*, Washington, DC: Belden, Russonello, and Stewart, 2000.

affected. The possible discrepancies between teacher-reported changes and student outcomes also highlights the fact that changes in input don't always produce changes in output.

Standards have proved controversial because they sometimes go beyond simple educational goals and become embroiled in disputes about the best methods of instruction. Although at first glance developing standards appears a straightforward process, in reality it is difficult and political because of ambiguous goals and disagreement over what makes effective teaching. With diffuse goals, differences of opinion on what and how to teach become the source of intense battles. For example, controversies over math instruction have involved a perceived dichotomy between the importance of knowing basic math operations and the need to have broad conceptual knowledge. Although each is clearly important, various curricula and approaches to mathematics instruction have tended to place more weight on one over the other, leading to conflicts over standards.

Measurement. The biggest controversy in accountability, however, probably surrounds how standards compliance should be measured. Proving that the standards have been met requires some sort of measurement. Assessing compliance requires several decisions: who to measure, what approach to use, how to create valid indices, and, frequently, where to set the critical value or cut-point for meeting the standard.

The centerpiece of current state accountability systems is the testing of student performance. This performance is then aggregated to, say, the school or district level, and some summary of the test scores is made public.

Though obvious, it is important to note first that direct assessment of performance focuses on students. Consistent with the goals and standards related to learning, all fifty states test students. Other influential parties, such as governors, legislatures, parents, and state boards of education, are currently excluded from direct performance measurement, even though they affect the ways schools behave and the ways students perform.[11] As discussed below, translation of student test results into measurement of performance for other participants is central to the incentives provided by various accountability systems.

A key issue in choosing valid test items is whether the material that is captured by a given standard can be directly translated into a test format. The dilemma lies less in the testability of content than in the feasibility of applying some independent scale of measurement to it. Some crude evidence about the movement in this direction is found from the use of criterion-referenced assessment, assessments that are designed to align closely with the learning standards and curriculum.[12] Forty-five states use criterion-referenced assessment in English, forty-three in mathematics, twenty-three in history/social studies (largely in middle and high schools), and twenty-nine in science.[13] The capacity of the various state criterion-referenced tests to capture existing standards has, however, not been generally assessed.

Another ongoing policy debate involves the mechanics of performance measurement. The mapping of standards to either observable or measurable dimensions necessarily requires abstraction and thus carries a degree of (unknown) error. Current tools used for students and/or teacher testing

----

[11]Teachers are frequently evaluated in a variety of ways, although this evaluation is seldomly systematically related to student performance and to state accountability systems. Teachers are also frequently tested, but this testing is designed to screen who gets into teaching. Thirty-nine states use tests on content knowledge for beginning teachers. No state has elected to test teachers periodically during their careers. Whether the current preservice testing improves student performance depends on the quality of the test as a predictor of performance, something that remains uncertain. See John M. Goff, *A More Comprehensive Accountability Model*, Washington, DC: Council for Basic Education, 2000.

[12]Criterion-referenced tests are frequently scored in terms of what percentage of the curriculum is mastered by the student. The common alternative is norm-referenced tests, which provide information on how well students do in comparison to a reference group of students and which are not as directly linked to any specific curriculum.

[13]"Quality Counts 2001: A Better Balance," *Education Week*.

include multiple-choice standardized tests, observational studies, expert assessments of portfolios of work, essay or other examples of written work, or short-answer tests. The options involve different tradeoffs in reliability, validity, ease of administration, and cost, but at this point in the evolution of accountability systems, not enough is known of the errors for various types of measurements or their distributional characteristics.[14]

The testing techniques used by states are presented in Table 2. Forty-nine states use standardized tests with multiple-choice format. Fewer states, thirty-eight, add short-answer questions to the testing format. Essays are used primarily for assessing English compositional skills in all but four states. Only two states, Vermont and Kentucky, employ the intensive method of assessing portfolios of student work.

States are not, however, always content with relying exclusively on outcome measures. Many states add in other factors, such as attendance rates (nine states), drop-out rates (fourteen states), or patterns of course enrollment (three states), when assessing the performance of schools. Use of these latter measures appears less directly related to outcome standards than test measures (although they may enter into the diagnosis of what is behind test performance).

Deriving Composite Measures.   While most of the public attention has gone to the development of standards and how to measure compliance with them, the use of resulting data, particularly when there are multiple objectives, is equally important. The goal of an accountability system is improving student performance, but performance is the outcome of a variety of factors: student ability and effort,

---

[14]A final decision in measurement typically is to determine the score that will be treated as the break between passing and failing. The choice is in one sense completely arbitrary; that is, choosing "70 out of 100" as the cut-point is more selective than "60 out of 100" but cannot be related in any systematic way to the underlying measures and metrics. And because it relies on aggregate test information, the choice of a cut-point cannot address any weaknesses or limitations in the underlying measures.

TABLE 2

Choice of Testing Items Used to Assess Students
(Value is number of states using method)

	Multiple Choice	Short Answer	Essay Answer	Portfolio of Work
Elementary School	49	36	44	2
Middle School	49	35	44	2
High School	48	28	43	2

Source: Author's tabulations from *Education Week* (2001).

parental inputs, teacher inputs, and school programs and resources. Even with accurate and reliable data on student performance, the outcome statistics produced must reflect the actions of the relevant people if they are to enter appropriately into performance incentives.

The issue of disentangling underlying elements of performance is most frequently raised in assessing the performance of teachers and schools. If we take accountability down to each of these levels, it is common sense that nobody should be held responsible for bad performance by others. For example, if a teacher starts with low-performing students but does a terrific job of improving their performance, she should not be penalized if the resulting performance level is still lower than, say, the national average. Similarly, a teacher starting with a high-performing group should get credit for her job in improving them but not for their initial preparation. The implication is that any measurement of teacher quality should focus on the teacher's addition, or value added, to student learning—and this requires adjusting the measurement of student performance according to the initial preparation of students. Similar arguments can be made that student accountability should focus on the gains of students after allowing for differences in the quality of teachers.

The best way to separate the different factors that influence student performance is currently unclear. A variety of approaches have been proposed and experimented with in the states. The most obvious starting measure—applied in virtually every existing accountability system—is the average of all student test scores for a district or a school. This aggregate summary, however, mixes all sources of performance. Other alternatives proposed and used in different places include:

- Annual change in school average score over time

- Average of the mean individual gains in scores

- Average scores of a school relative to state average scores for students of similar background

- Regression adjusted scores to remove individual background differences

The list could be extended, but these illustrate that performance measurement can take many forms. Importantly, as discussed below, these derived measures differ in the degree to which they reveal the contribution of the underlying factors and thus in their value in developing good incentive systems.

These measures also highlight a fundamental tension between the incentives that are created by the way a given accountability system is structured and the overall performance goals they are supposed to promote. For example, for many incentive uses it may be desirable to pinpoint the value added by each school, but even a high-value-added school may start with students sufficiently ill-prepared so that the school does not bring them up to the desired levels of student performance. Looked at from the viewpoint of enforcing high standards of student performance, this school might be judged as falling short—though from the incentive side, this school would deserve praise. This apparently simple issue illustrates the difficulties of using student performance data simultaneously for multiple goals. A common approach is for states to create incentives involving a combination of the level of score and the school change in score over time (such as seen in school reward systems in North Carolina and California). Nonetheless, such approaches, though recognizing a range of measures, may still not align the measurement and incentives appropriately.

Finally, the possibilities for deriving value-added measures relate directly to the choice of measurement approach. Given the current level of inexperience, it is important not to exclude the ability to examine performance from multiple vantage points. For example, as discussed below, the methods that are best suited for tracking teacher and school performance appear to be ones that track the performance change of individual students over time. This approach can control better for ability and background differences across students, which bias simple aggregates that do not consider variations in the cohorts being assessed. But tracking individuals over time cannot be done in systems that use sporadic testing (e.g., those testing only fourth, eighth, and twelfth graders). Moreover, testing regimes that involve portfolios of work, though subject to reliability concerns at any point in time, generally defy consideration of growth in performance over time.[15]

Reporting. Report cards for schools are prepared and published in forty-five states, but the calculations differ widely, making comparisons impossible. In addition, thirty-four states are also producing a district-level report. Two additional states will join the school report card practice in the future, leaving Idaho and Montana the only states that provide no public information on the performance of their education efforts.

To help the public interpret the statistics, seventeen states (with another six planning to) have created aggregate ratings systems of available outcome information and/or input data. Another ten states (with two more in the next few years) use ratings only to identify poor-performing schools. In both practices, however, additional information may be incorporated into the rating, at the state's discretion. Table 3 shows the types of information that states use to rate their schools.

[15]Cf. Daniel Koretz, Brian Stecher, Stephen Klein, Daniel McCaffrey, and Edward Deibert, "Can Portfolios Assess Student Performance and Influence Instruction: The 1991–92 Vermont Experience," CSE Technical Report 371, Rand Institute on Education and Training, 1993.

Many states that incorporate multiple measurements into their ratings do not explain the breakdown, so we are unable to judge which ratings accurately reflect school performance. The lack of computational transparency and consistency could lead to future problems when consequences are attached to performance.

Uses and Consequences.[16]   Goals, standards, and measurements create an accountability system. But the mechanics of such a system are largely unrelated to the way states put the results to use.

In most states, accountability systems have multiple objectives—including creating a measuring rod for outcomes, improving school instruction, creating incentives, and creating rewards/punishments for performance.

The standards and accountability movement strives to induce alignment among standards, teaching, and student performance. In contrast to a regulatory approach, the underlying philosophy of accountability is letting the responsible parties maintain control of a process whose outcomes are scrutinized. Consequences—both positive and negative—are the fulcrum that gives leverage to the other players in the education system. If schools or students do not expect any decisive actions as a result of their performance, there is little to motivate attention to the outcomes they produce.

The clearest use of performance standards is to judge student accomplishments. Test scores are used as a graduation requirement in eighteen states (with another six to follow suit in the next three years). Three states use test scores as a promotional criterion from grade to grade. Students with high performance are eligible for scholarships in six states.

The picture with respect to other uses is less clear. Before the movement to greater usage of formal accountability

---

[16]See the compilation in "Quality Counts 2001: A Better Balance," *Education Week*.

TABLE 3

Information Used by States to Create School Ratings

Source of Information	Number of States Using Source
Student test scores only	14
Multiple sources:	
Test scores/drop-out rates	4
Test scores/drop-out rates/other	1
Test scores/attendance	1
Test scores/drop-out rates/attendance	2
Test scores/drop-out rates/attendance/other	7

Source: Author's tabulations from *Education Week* (2001).

systems, many states were accustomed to making judgments about individual school and district performance. All told, 5,613 schools were identified as low performing in the 1999–2000 school year—with many almost certainly making this list primarily because of the average level of student test performance.[17] Many of these, however, were not the result of newly adopted accountability systems. With the advent of new accountability systems and ratings (as shown in Table 3), these judgments are likely to become more systematic.

Creating incentives for schools and teachers is more complicated than creating them for students. Perhaps due to the newness of the policy, accountability systems across the country rely primarily on rewards for good performance or significant improvement. The snapshot of possibilities and actions in the 2001 school year is instructive. For example, twenty states reward schools, and sixteen give teacher bonuses for good performance. Far fewer states, however, impose sanctions. Only fourteen states are authorized to close, reconstitute, or take over a failing school. Of those states, only four have actually followed through with consequences, in a total of seventy schools. Sixteen states are

---

[17]Ibid.

permitted to replace teachers or principals, but only two cases have been pursued. Just nine states allow students in consistently poor-performing schools to enroll in other schools; widespread court challenges have delayed this option in other states. Clearly, if Florida courts ultimately uphold the A+ program (which permits students in schools that twice receive failing ratings to enroll elsewhere), more schools will likely exercise this option. Eleven states are authorized to revoke accreditation. However, because accreditation can be reinstated with plans to improve—instead of on proven performance—this option is not considered as strong a consequence as others. Only Texas reports using students' test scores to evaluate their teachers.

Incentives and the Application of Accountability Data

The effectiveness of accountability systems rests on three legs: standards, measurement, and consequences. Yet at the most fundamental level, the relationship between these three things is frequently ignored. Consider who is being judged. The most common direct incentives built into state accountability systems revolve around student requirements. As described, about half of the states have consequential test requirements for students, and others are sure to follow. However, few have been binding yet because of phase-in requirements and test experimentation. This aspect of learning has been well documented, although the impact of differing performance requirements on student achievement is less well understood.[18]

---

[18]The importance of student incentives has been most thoroughly developed by John Bishop (e.g., John Bishop, "Signaling, Incentives, and School Organization in France, the Netherlands, Britain, and United States," in *Improving America's Schools: The Role of Incentives,* Eric A. Hanushek and Dale W. Jorgenson, editors, Washington, DC: National Academy Press, 1996). He argues that external testing leads to significant changes in the motivation of students in their subsequent effort and results. Nonetheless, the best form of such incentives in the context of state accountability systems requires further attention.

But though accountability systems create direct incentives for students, they produce only indirect ones for schools and teachers.[19] Accountability systems work well only if they provide a direct link between outcomes and the behavior of each person in question. Thus, consequences for teachers must be directly related to their effect on student performance. If related to overall levels of student performance, the system would obviously be unfair for teachers who worked with students entering their classrooms with large deficits. They would be punished for something outside of their control. Instead of promoting better performance by teachers, such a system might be expected to have more significant effects on the choices of schools by teachers. Improper measurement can break the link between actions and consequences.

These issues have led to the various approaches delineated, both academic and governmental, to produce reliable estimates of the value added of different schools. The previous discussion of test measures provided a partial listing of the choices currently being made. Nonetheless, even though several states report alternatives and actually issue school rewards based on them, the properties of alternative approaches are not completely understood.

Measurement Accuracy

Some obvious concerns have been raised in previous discussions about accountability, but they have yet to be resolved. For example, the high level of student mobility across schools means that cohort changes over time can have significant effects on measured performance when individual student gains are not considered. For perspective,

---

[19]Some argue that if students are finding it difficult or impossible to pass the required tests, pressures will be placed on schools that will lead to their improvement. These pressures might be self-generated by school personnel who wish to do a good job, come from school boards and parents, or be the result of Tiebout pressures from school district choices. Little analysis is available to show the strength of such indirect incentives.

in Texas schools, one-third of the students will change schools between grades 4 and 7 (after eliminating all structural moves associated with moving to middle schools from elementary schools). These moves are also more frequent for low-income and minority students.[20] Similarly, mobility of teachers and principals makes it difficult to infer who is responsible for any performance changes of schools over time. For example, average teacher movements in the mid-1990s in Texas show that less than 80 percent of the teachers in any given year remain at the school they were in the prior year.[21] Thus, any simple comparisons of school average scores over time yield ambiguous performance information.

Measurement errors in individual tests can also lead to score changes for small schools over time without being related to any fundamental differences in performance.[22] This presents a dilemma, since error can be reduced by averaging over time, but such averaging makes it difficult to pinpoint any performance changes. And different adjustment methods, such as those previously identified, lead to differing rankings without any clear superiority in terms of true differences in school performance.[23]

These issues also introduce a dilemma. In order to emphasize performance of schools in elevating scores of poor and minority children, states have both required reporting of disaggregated scores and moved to link reward to such distributional information. But scores disaggregated by sub-

---

[20]Eric A. Hanushek, John F. Kain, and Steve G. Rivkin, "Disruption Versus Tiebout Improvement: The Costs and Benefits of Switching Schools," Cambridge, MA: National Bureau of Economic Research, 2001.

[21]Eric A. Hanushek, John F. Kain, and Steve G. Rivkin, "Why Public Schools Lose Teachers," Cambridge, MA: National Bureau of Economic Research, 2001.

[22]Thomas J. Kane and Douglas O. Staiger, "Improving School Accountability Measures," Cambridge, MA: National Bureau of Economic Research, 2001.

[23]Charles T. Clotfelter and Helen F. Ladd, "Recognizing and Rewarding Success in Public Schools," in Holding Schools Accountable: Performance-Based Reform in Education, Helen F. Ladd, editor, Washington, DC: Brookings Institute Press, 1996, pp. 23–63.

populations necessarily involve smaller numbers of students and thus are more subject to random measurement errors. Balancing these requires not only care in the design of incentives but also detailed technical considerations that go beyond just the goals of the system.

A further issue, which extends the previous concerns about separating sources of performance, is the use of derived measures to assess individual teacher performance. The growing databases in states on annual school performance permit measurement of student achievement gains that are directly related to individual teachers.[24] Again, many of the issues raised about school accounting are relevant but more severe here because of the smaller numbers of students involved in the performance measurement.

Using Single-Cut Scores

The strength of incentives is affected by the standards and measurement. It seems natural to many to judge performance as meeting standards or not, that is, to define an acceptable level of knowledge. Obviously, the determination of the passing score is somewhat arbitrary and has a variety of political ramifications. Without going into details about those, the important point here is that differing cutoffs for passing can produce some undesirable incentives. Systems based on raising students over an absolute passing score cause schools and teachers to focus more on students close to the cut-score—because those are the students who can usually be moved across the boundary most easily. At the

---

[24]Rivkin, Hanushek, and Kain show how teacher quality can be separated from student factors by using panel data on different cohorts of students (Steven G. Rivkin, Eric A. Hanushek, and John F. Kain, "Teachers, Schools, and Academic Achievement," Cambridge, MA: National Bureau of Economic Research [revised], 2001). The state of Tennessee has actually implemented an alternative approach to identifying individual teacher impacts and uses this in its internal school management. See William L. Sanders and Sandra P. Horn, "The Tennessee Value-Added Assessment System (TVAAS): Mixed-Model Methodology in Educational Assessment," *Journal of Personnel Evaluation in Education* 8, 1994: 299–311.

same time, the cutoff weakens the incentive to work with students far below or far above the cutoff.[25] This problem becomes especially acute when considering heterogeneous populations. For such populations, it is very difficult to set absolute cutoffs that don't unfairly penalize disadvantaged and minority students, who more frequently begin with poor performance. At the same time, failing to reward higher-performing students would also render the accountability system ineffective.

Heterogeneous Populations

Inherent in our current organization of education is the assumption that all students can progress at roughly the same pace. The choice of passing score marks the "finish line" that all students are expected to cross in a given year. But the real world presents a different picture. Dealing with passing scores in states or districts with very heterogeneous populations introduces fundamental difficulties of both a political and a conceptual nature. From the political side, there are tensions between having stringent and demanding standards and the need to deal fairly with different populations. It is politically unacceptable to leave disadvantaged or minority students behind, but as currently constructed, many of the accountability systems do just that in their efforts to be challenging to higher-performing students. As long as we continue to expect homogeneous rates of progress in absolute time

---

[25]The implications of such incentives based on passing scores can be seen from prior work on "performance contracting." In an effort to understand the potential of contracting with private employers to provide remedial education, the Office of Economic Opportunity attempted an experiment. The contract, which provided no payment for any student performing below grade level and a ceiling on the largest payment, led several private providers to ignore both the poorest and best performing students (see Edward M. Gramlich and Patricia P. Koshel, *Educational Performance Contracting*, Washington, DC: The Brookings Institute Press, 1975). More recent observations of this kind are made for Texas by Deere and Strayer (Donald Deere and Wayne Strayer, "Putting Schools to the Test: School Accountability, Incentives, and Behavior," Department of Economics, Texas A&M University, 2001).

frames, we will hinder our ability to address differences in starting points or rates of progress. Just as schools are left to find the best way to achieve the performance measures set for them, we may also eventually consider greater flexibility for students in reaching the performance standards set for them.

The conceptual issues involve the uses and interpretation of the measurements in the accountability system. The system can be used simply to identify levels of student performance and signal to others—employers, colleges, and the like—who is below the cutoff at a given point in time. It can also be used to separately provide incentives for higher performance. As Betts and Costrell demonstrate, these alternate uses lead to some unexpected outcomes when they interact with varying cutoffs in heterogeneous populations.[26] In particular, the different uses can conflict, requiring a clearer delineation of goals and objectives.

One implication of consideration of passing scores is that the binary nature of the scores leads to a set of complications that are avoided by simply providing more detailed information about the distribution of underlying scores, as opposed to relying on just "pass" and "fail." Although such a system does not have the same political appeal, it does permit both information about overall performance and good incentives to students to coexist.

This issue, of course, has different implications when considering accountability based on value added for teachers and schools. The development of passing scores and the building of incentives on them applies most directly to consideration of overall level of scores. If, on the other hand, the system assesses how far a teacher moves a student toward the standards, the cutoffs have less important implications. Concentrating on the reporting of score levels could facilitate the assessment and reward/punishment of teachers, for

---

[26]Julian R. Betts and Robert M. Costrell, "Incentives and Equity under Standards-Based Reform," in *Brookings Papers on Education Policy: 2001*, Diane Ravitch, editor, Washington, DC: Brookings Institute Press, 2001.

it could track how far a teacher moves a student toward standards. Cutoffs, therefore, would have fewer political dilemmas. One option may be to set fixed standards for diplomas or graduation but permit flexible time frames for meeting them, with the accountability and incentive systems looking at how schools and teachers contribute to progress over time. Nonetheless, in order to provide incentives in different parts of the performance distribution, some sort of "enhanced diploma" would still be useful.

SOME ISSUES OF IMPLEMENTATION

The newness of strong accountability systems leaves individual states to make guesses about what is best. It also opens up larger political problems.

Feasibility. The political nature of the standards and accountability process leads to huge tensions. No state wishes to be known for setting standards that are too low or that can be construed as not challenging. On the other hand, standards that are too high become infeasible—and could involve serious harm, depending on the consequences for not meeting them.

Consider the actions of the state of New York. In 1999, the Board of Regents decided that it should do away with lower levels of diplomas and require all students to obtain its premier diploma, the Regents diploma. The Regents diploma requires passing a series of rigorous subject-area examinations that are linked to a difficult underlying curriculum. At the time of development of this standard, some 40 percent of graduating high school students in the state obtained Regents diplomas. Twenty-one percent of graduating students in New York City obtained a Regents diploma. Simply mandating that all students move to the new standard is likely to leave many who previously would have received some sort of diploma without a diploma—arguably a very harmful situation. The hope of the new standard is that it would lead students to work harder and would lead schools to do a better job. On the other hand, it also looks generally infeasible under the new standard for the school systems in many parts of New York State, most particularly for New York City, to obtain graduation rates close to those previously achieved.

One response, followed by New York State, is to stretch out the time period before the standards are applied. Thus, though they originally were to be operative today, the phase-in period has been extended into the future. Whether this will permit full phase-in depends on how well school systems can respond (i.e., on whether the goals move closer to being feasible). Currently, this possibility is unclear.

The Need for Both Rewards and Sanctions. The incentives that derive from the design and use of accountability systems work only to the extent that they motivate students, teachers, and schools to examine their performance and make changes to improve, if necessary. Without consequences, incentives disappear. But people will react to consequences differently. Some are motivated positively by bonuses, whereas others find them offensive. Some people, but not all, are only moved by the wish to avoid negative consequences. Relying solely on rewards may not be sufficient to overcome the inertia of habit; but likewise, the existence of only sanctions can demoralize and undermine sustained effort. This suggests that accountability systems should acknowledge different patterns of motivation and incorporate these differences into the design. Having both negative and positive consequences creates avoidance incentives and attraction incentives and can address more fully the range of motivations. As the previous state data suggest, nonetheless, most school incentives are currently heavily weighted toward rewards.

Testing the Premises. At the outset, it is important to recognize that there is little experience in the design and operation of educational accountability systems and their elements. In many ways, this does not differ from many other educational policies that are introduced more on superficial plausibility than on any evidence. As an example, there is uncertainty about how schools and teachers react to the incentives introduced. If the implicit weights in the incentive system favor a certain set of subjects at the expense of others, does it lead to undesirable distortions in the balance of teaching? Does the incentive structure lead to cooperation among the teachers? Does it change the amount of teacher turnover?

One implication of this is that states must be prepared to review and revise as experience reveals better information about the underlying linkages. But the ways that states go about these important steps introduce potential problems that need mentioning.

There is a distinct trade-off between adjusting incentives and maintaining a strong set of incentives. School personnel today are accustomed to frequently changing programs and perspectives of schools, leading to some cynicism about the staying power of any innovation. Accountability systems also face unique problems of adjustments going beyond those of normal programs. Many of the potential adjustments that are feasible are long-term responses—reflecting better selection and motivation of teachers, improved student effort, better matching of students and programs, and the like. In order for incentives to elicit these long-term impacts, the participants must believe that the incentives will remain in place over the long term. But balanced against this is the difficulty in designing incentive structures given our current knowledge.

We do not know much about how best to accumulate knowledge or even about which directions schools might take to improve. Some hope comes from other states. With so many states launching these systems at about the same time, states can look to each other to learn from their similarities and differences without each needing to continuously vary their own design.

Ensuring That Accountability Systems Effect Change

Once an accountability system is in place, there are still many things that need to be done to ensure it actually produces change. Some of these things, which bring up further unresolved issues, are discussed below.

Dealing with Poor Performance. Consequences for poor performance are far from straightforward. What many fail to realize in the context of accountability systems is that appropriate consequences vary according to the causes of bad performance. For example, if deficient student background is the determining factor, simply increasing school resources may be the answer; if, on the other hand, poor performance is due to poor teaching, a different solution is required. Many people tend to assume that all poor performance by students is either one or the other: poor preparation that must be compensated for or bad teaching and school management. In reality, observed poor performance almost certainly has elements of each, if not in individual schools, at least across different schools. Accountability schemes must not continue to ignore this fundamental issue, for it has important consequences for program design.

The correct answer requires sufficient evidence to distinguish the causes of poor performance. Though this is largely an implication of prior discussions about aligning results with the people responsible for each of the components, it has obvious importance to overall design issues. And the current systems have not been demonstrated to be effective at this.

Incentives and Efficiency. To return to the motivation for accountability systems in the first place, namely that student performance has remained flat while resources have grown dramatically, one of the unanswered questions of the new accountability systems is the degree to which they yield efficiency gains through the incentives they create. Will incentives to improve student achievement outputs naturally lead to better use of resources? The answer is not obvious.

Although a simple version would be that schools redirect their resources to the places of highest payoffs, this cannot be assumed. For example, if the largest incentive and impact of incentives comes through student effort, there might be little impact on efficiency of resource usage. Or if the direct incentives for teachers and school personnel are less than the value they put on current resource usage, there might be little impact on efficiency. This latter case could arise, say, where teachers take extra resources in terms of greater free time and where the individual benefit of any incentive reward is less than their valuation of the free time.

Again, little is known about any collateral impact of accountability structures and their resulting incentives on the efficiency of resource usage. The impact will clearly vary with the magnitude of incentives, the ease of achieving desired outputs, and the alternative uses of resources.

Knowing Performance Is Poor Is Different from Knowing What to Do.   Even though the purpose of accountability systems is to improve student learning, how exactly to achieve this faces several dilemmas. Accountability systems identify when things are not working well but not what corrective actions are required. In fact, an accountability system operates on the assumption that assuring good performance is something that cannot be regulated at the state level—for different schools require different solutions. The situation is further compounded by the fact that teacher quality studies suggest that the key to effective improvement may be changes in personnel, as opposed to the programmatic fixes currently focused on training and support of current teachers.[27]

The dilemma is clear. Though some schools may know how to solve their problems, others may have no idea, and past research has produced no clear indication of what precisely

---

[27]See, for example, Rivkin, Hanushek, and Kain, "Teachers, Schools, and Academic Achievement," Cambridge, MA: National Bureau of Economic Research, 2001.

helps students learn. Continuing research into the determinants of performance may be part of the answer, but so far such research has yet to be successful, and it is unlikely to provide any immediate guidance. This inherent and potentially serious weakness must be recognized.

Thus, a key element of the move to direct accountability is a presumption that local people, with incentives and motivation, will be best positioned to improve student outcomes. Clearly, this presumption needs to be judged over time. Evaluating this presumption should be a top priority of accountability systems.

External Validity. One of the largest issues facing accountability systems is also one of the most basic. Ideally, tests and incentives should align with a school's learning objectives. At the same time, a system that is not geared to ultimate users—higher education and the job market—cannot be very productive.

All current testing is focused on meeting an initial set of standards that are assumed to reflect the set of knowledge that adequately prepares students for their postschooling years. There is surprisingly little attempt to match this with subsequent performance. The research on this is also quite thin. There is increasing research suggesting that performance on cognitive tests is strongly related to labor market earnings, but this research has not been very careful in distinguishing among alternative performance measures (and their underlying standards of knowledge).

CONCLUSIONS

Within the past quarter of a century, the desire to improve student performance has caused policymakers to focus directly on student achievement. Although prior policy has focused almost exclusively on what's going into the educational system, recent reforms have shifted the focus to what's coming out—what we want students to know and how we can be sure they know it. The accountability systems now being put in place are an attempt to ensure that the goals for student knowledge are actually accomplished. The simple structure of current accountability systems, however, masks how its elements interact in a complex fashion that can produce unexpected outcomes.

Current accountability systems revolve around measured student performance, even though student performance is influenced not only by students but also by parents, teachers, and schools. Concentrating on student performance is a very important and positive change in how we view schools. Nonetheless, although the movement toward performance-based systems offers the best chance for improvement, the journey has just begun.[28] The focus on improving outcomes should be applied with equal rigor to educational perform-ance and to the accountability systems themselves. The challenge is harnessing this fundamental movement to bring about the desired changes.

---

[28]Eric A. Hanushek and others, *Making Schools Work: Improving Performance and Controlling Costs*, Washington, DC: Brookings Institute Press, 1994.

State Accountability Systems

Lance T. Izumi and Williamson M. Evers

For years, proposals for reforming education have centered on increasing inputs, such as more funding for teacher salaries, school construction, and computer equipment. However, with the public disappointed at the lack of major improvement in student performance (despite rising government education budgets), lawmakers have shifted their emphasis to making sure that schools are accountable for the results they produce. As a consequence, many states have created accountability systems that are supposed to ensure that schools in general—and teachers, principals, and district officials in particular—focus on improving student achievement. These accountability programs, however, vary widely both in the means by which they hold schools accountable and in the effectiveness of those means.

State accountability systems are made up of the state academic content standards, the state's tests, and the rewards and sanctions for performance. Whether an accountability

The authors wish to thank Paul Clopton, Jay Greene, Chris Patterson, and Bill Lucia for having read an earlier draft of this paper and for providing suggestions for improvement. They also wish to thank Diallo Dphrepaulezz and Kate Feinstein for research assistance.

system is effective depends on how good these components are and how well they work together.

Margaret Goertz, co-director of the Consortium for Policy Research in Education at the University of Pennsylvania and co-author of a recent report on accountability systems, poses five questions that should be addressed in order to evaluate accountability systems.[1] First, what are schools accountable for? Policymakers must decide what they want to measure, whether it is knowledge of basic skills, attendance and dropout rates, or other indices of performance. Second, for whom are schools accountable? Policymakers must decide whether to hold schools accountable for the performance of all students or to exclude learning-disabled students and non-English-speaking students. Third, does the accountability system measure progress absolutely or relatively? Policymakers must decide whether a set standard must be met (such as a set test score) or whether it is sufficient to show relative progress over time. Fourth, is the accountability system fair? Policymakers need to ensure that all subgroups of students improve their performance. Finally, is the accountability system informative?[2] For example, testing information must be timely and understandable.

Goertz says that there are three characteristics of successful accountability systems. Such systems encourage schools and districts to have curriculum and teaching that are in line with state standards, to analyze testing data and make use of it in teaching practices, and to make sure students are continuing to make progress year after year.[3] According to Goertz, research is showing that school staff want to work

---

[1] "National Accountability Movement Offers Lessons for California," Palo Alto, CA: EdSource, May 2000: 2–7. This report is an account of the March 2000 EdSource conference on "Ranking California Schools: Will It Improve Student Learning? Undermine Public Support?"

[2] On the importance of information for accountability, see Caroline M. Hoxby, "Testing Is About Openness and Openness Works," Hoover Institution Weekly Essays, July 30, 2001, <http://www.hoover.stanford.edu/pubaffairs/we/current/hoxby_0701.html>.

[3] "National Accountability Movement," 7.

in "more focused ways" on state and district goals because of accountability systems' "positive and negative consequences."[4]

There are other important questions. For instance, if the accountability system is based on state academic content standards, how good are the standards and how aligned are tests with the standards? Also, do the rewards and sanctions really provide an incentive for individual students, teachers, and administrators to improve performance?

The rest of this chapter will apply these various criteria to a sample group of state accountability systems. The chapter looks at California, Texas, and Florida because journalists and policy analysts have said that these states have either comprehensive or innovative accountability programs or both. These three states have accountability programs that are better than those in most other states. Yet the real question that this chapter considers is whether these programs are likely to be effective in improving student achievement.

CALIFORNIA

In April 1999, California passed the Public Schools Accountability Act, the brainchild of newly elected Governor Gray Davis. This accountability law has three major components. First, the Academic Performance Index was to provide individual schools with a numerical score based originally on multiple measures of performance (e.g., test scores, dropout rates, and attendance rates) but which is now, for the time being, based exclusively on student test scores. Second, the rewards program (called the High Performing-Improving Schools Program) would award schools and staff monetary bonuses if they met or surpassed Academic Performance Index growth targets. The third component was the intervention program (called the Immediate Intervention-Underperforming Schools Pro-

---

[4]Ibid.

gram). The state would intervene in schools that failed to meet targets for improvement in test scores. The intervention-program portion of the legislation also included sanctions (such as state takeover of individual schools) and grants to pay for the interventions.

At present, the state calculates the Academic Performance Index using only scores from the Stanford-9 standardized test. The State Board of Education chose the Stanford-9, which is a multiple-choice, norm-referenced examination, to be the state's assessment device in 1997, several years before passage of the new accountability law. The board chose this test, in part, because as an "off-the-shelf" exam, it was readily available. The state uses the Stanford-9 to test grades 2–11, with students in grades 2–8 tested in reading, mathematics, written expression, and spelling. Students in grades 9–11 are tested in reading, writing, mathematics, science, and history and social science. All students at each grade level take the exact same Stanford-9 exam, and the state requires districts to provide individual student scores to parents. The state Department of Education's Web site publicly lists aggregate Stanford-9 scores by grade level for schools, districts, counties, and the state.

As part of a high-stakes accountability system, such as California's system, the Stanford-9 is less than optimal because it is not aligned to the state's academic content standards.[5] The state picked out parts of the Stanford-9 that tested the topics listed in the content standards and also developed a set of standards-aligned questions that were added onto the Stanford-9 exam. Later the state expanded this approach into separate standards-based tests (the California Standards Tests). The state gives standards-based tests in reading and mathematics in grades 2–11. Students in

---

[5]Compare Barbara Miller of EdSource, quoted in Erika Chavez, "High School Test Scores Stagnant: Frustrated Educators Are Trying to Figure Out Why Teens Aren't Doing Better," *Sacramento Bee*, August 17, 2001.

grades 4 and 7 are tested on writing, and those in grades 9–11 are tested on the state content standards in science and in history and social science.[6] Students' performance on these standards-based questions have not yet become part of the Performance Index calculation, although they will be included in coming years.

In the future, California plans to retain the Stanford-9 (or an equivalent nationally normed test) both as a "basic skills" test and as a check on how California's self-assessed progress measures up against national norms of performance.[7] But in 2002, the state will shift emphasis away from the Stanford-9 and will rely mainly on its standards-based tests for accountability. These tests reflect the state's 1997–98 academic content standards, which California educational officials, California school teachers, and national experts alike consider to be quite high, probably the highest in the country.[8]

But thus far the state has exclusively used Stanford-9 for accountability. In addition to this test not being based on the state standards, there is another drawback to using it as a tool of accountability. Stanford-9 questions do not change from year to year.[9] As the state Legislative Analyst's Office, the nonpartisan research arm of the State Legislature, points out, "Particularly with a high stakes test, it is important to vary test questions from year to year in order to minimize possibilities for literal 'teaching

---

[6]In late 2001, the State Board of Education announced plans for a history test in grade 8 (and elimination of the current history test in grade 9) as well as a science test in grade 5.

[7]Suzanne Tachney in David Fleishhacker and Tacheny, "Arguments: Do Tests Add Up?" *San Francisco Chronicle*, September 2, 2001; Larry Crabbe, quoted in Erika Chavez, "School Test Results Out This Week," *Sacramento Bee*, August 13, 2001.

[8]Tachney in Fleishhacker and Tacheny; Erika Chavez, "Kids Fare Poorly on New Test: Just Three in 10 Meet the State's Standards in Language Arts," *Sacramento Bee*, August 16, 2001.

[9]In contrast, the California Standards Tests are "refreshed" with a significant proportion of new questions each year.

to the test' and outright cheating."[10] With increasing fre-
quency, schools have used bootlegged copies of the test,
and officials have had to discipline school personnel for
cheating.

When questions do not change from year to year, test scores
tend to rise each year as students become more familiar with
the sort of questions on the test. Increasing scores may not,
therefore, represent increases in true learning but rather test
preparation and gaming strategies. According to Joan
Herman, co-director of the Center for Research on Evaluation, Standards, and Student Testing at UCLA, scores usually
drop when test writers introduce new questions or forms and
then rise again as the test becomes more familiar.[11] Says
Herman, testing specialists concur that "it's not a good idea to
give the same test form from year to year, or use exactly
the same test items."[12] "By changing test forms or changing
the items," says Herman, "you prevent schools from over-
focusing on the specific items that are on the test."[13]

For 2000–2001, though, the Academic Performance Index
used only the Stanford-9 scores and did not use any scores
from the augmented standards-aligned tests. Based on the
Stanford-9 results, the state Department of Education calculates a score ranging from a low of 200 to a high of 1,000
for each school. The interim statewide Academic Performance Index target for all schools is 800. The state Department of Education also ranked schools on a one-to-ten
decile ranking scale, with ten being the best. The department uses a separate "similar schools" ranking to compare
schools with other schools having similar demographic
characteristics.

---

[10]"Analysis of the 2001–02 Budget Bill," Sacramento, CA: Legislative Analyst's Office, February 2001: E-93.

[11]"California's Student Testing System: Hard Choices and New Direction," Palo
Alto, CA: EdSource, June 2001: 7. This report is an account of the April 2001 Ed-
Source forum on "Tests and More Tests: The Road Ahead for Student Assessment."

[12]Ibid.

[13]Ibid.

Because the Stanford-9 is a norm-referenced test, the state reports results also in terms of national percentiles. The state uses three performance levels or cut-points, the twenty-fifth, fiftieth, and seventy-fifth national percentiles, to create school, district, county, and state scores. The state does not use any further performance levels or criteria in reporting Stanford-9 results.

Schools scoring below 800 must close the gap between their current score and the state performance target by at least 5 percent to meet their growth target for the year. For example, if a school's 1999 Academic Performance Index score was 500, the school's growth target would be (800 − 500) × 5 percent = 15 points.[14] Yet with these growth targets, the state requires so little improvement that, for many schools, meeting the state's target score of 800 would take decades.

Each numerically significant ethnic or socioeconomically disadvantaged subgroup at a school (that constitutes at least 15 percent of the school's total pupil population and consists of at least thirty students) must have a growth target of 80 percent of the school's growth target. Thus, if a school's growth target was 15 points, each numerically significant subgroup at the school must improve by at least 80 percent of 15 points, that is, by 12 points.

The rewards portion of the accountability system includes several programs that are triggered when schools meet their growth targets and subgroup targets and have 95 percent Stanford-9 participation in grades K–8 and 90 percent participation in grades 9–11. One program, the Governor's Performance Awards, sends state grants to individual school-site councils, which have the discretion to use the funds as they see fit. In addition, state grants from the School Site Employee Performance Bonus Program are to be divided equally among school site councils and all school site staff. Finally, the Certificated Staff Performance Incentives Program targets staff at low-performing schools that have the

---

[14]The State Department of Education uses this example.

highest growth rates. The program awards $25,000 bonuses
to 1,000 staff statewide, $10,000 bonuses to 3,750 staff
members, and $5,000 bonuses to 7,500 staff members.

The intervention program originally applied to those
schools that scored below the fiftieth percentile on the
Stanford-9. More than 3,100 schools fell into this cate-
gory. The state changed the program in 2000. Now
schools that rank in the lower half of the Academic Performance Index and fail to meet their growth targets are
eligible to apply to receive state interventionary assistance.
Under these requirements, 938 schools were eligible. Once
eligible, however, not all low-performing schools become
part of the intervention program. Participation is voluntary, and schools must apply. Once schools apply, state
officials select only 430 schools each year. As a result,
many low-performing schools neither apply nor are
selected for the program. For example, in 2000–2001, of
the 938 eligible schools, only 532 applied for the 430 slots.
In other words, 406 eligible low-scoring schools voluntarily decided not to apply, and of those that did, 102 were
not selected.

The upshot is that some of the worst schools in the state,
such as those ranked at the 1 level, are neither compelled
to apply for the program nor guaranteed selection if they do
apply. It is quite possible for a school with a 4 ranking to be
chosen over a school with a 1 ranking. Further, the school
with the lowest Academic Performance Index score in the
state may not be eligible for the program if it meets its incremental annual growth target.[15] Thus, such a school
would be ineligible to apply to the program, whereas a
higher scoring school may be eligible if the latter failed to
meet its growth target.

Once selected for the program, schools in the first year
receive $50,000 in planning grants to develop a comprehen-
sive school reform plan. As part of the planning phase,

---

[15]Legislative Analyst's Office, op. cit., E-101.

schools must hire qualified external evaluators to assist in developing the reform plans. The plan must then be approved by the state Board of Education. After approval, the school receives annual implementation grants of up to $200 per enrolled student. Schools receive the implementation grant for two years and may be granted a third year of funding if they continue to struggle to meet their Academic Performance Index growth targets.

A major weakness of the reform plan process is the lack of quality control over the recommendations made by the external evaluators. Some schools have complained that the external evaluators do little except put the ball in the court of teachers and principals to come up with a reform plan. Proponents of solid education have complained that all too many evaluators recommend progressive student-centered teaching methods—such as discovery learning—that, according to the evidence, do not improve student achievement.

Schools in the program that fail to meet their growth targets may be subject to a number of sanctions. If a school fails to meet its target but there is evidence of significant growth, the school can continue in the intervention program and continue to receive funding. If the school fails to meet its growth target in twelve months and doesn't show significant growth, state officials may reassign the staff, negotiate various site-specific changes, or try other approaches. If a school fails to meet growth targets and to show significant growth after twenty-four months, the state superintendent of public instruction may take over the school, reassign the principal, and, in addition, do one of the following:

- Allow students to attend other public schools
- Transform the school into a charter school
- Turn the management of the school over to another educational institution
- Reassign the teachers
- Negotiate a new labor contract

- Reorganize the school
- Close the school

In fall 2001, Governor Davis signed a bill that layers another state funding program on top of the existing intervention program. Under this funding program, low-performing schools could receive a grant of $400 per student—double the previous amount granted for implementation. However, instead of being subject to independent external evaluation, as is the case under the present intervention program, the new funding program allows districts to evaluate their own schools. Further, the sanctions timeline would be lengthened. Rather than face sanctions after two years, schools that fail to improve get another year to raise their performance (and this time only under district supervision). Even if they do not hit their annual testing growth target, schools can then get another year's reprieve if they simply show "significant" growth. It may be four or more years before any sanctions are imposed on failing schools.

Every year, local school boards must issue a School Accountability Report Card for each school within the district. Each report card must include the most recent three years of testing data for student achievement by grade level in reading, writing, arithmetic, and other academic goals. Secondary school report cards will also list the percentage of seniors taking the SAT college admissions test and their average grade on the test. Also reported are dropout rates and suspension and expulsion rates, plus progress toward reducing class size. Finally, the report cards list the number of days of staff development and the number of credentialed teachers, emergency credentialed teachers, teachers without credentials, and teachers working outside their areas of competence. The local board must send these accountability report cards to all parents.

Although not formally part of the 1999 accountability law, California has also created a High School Exit Exam (HSEE) aligned to the state's academic content standards.

The American Institutes for Research developed the test for the state, and it covers English-language arts through the tenth grade and math through Algebra I. The exam is graded on a pass-fail basis, and students in the class of 2004 must pass the exam to receive their high school diploma. In March 2001, about 350,000 high school freshmen took the HSEE for the first time. A state advisory committee recommended that the cut-point for a passing score be 70 percent. However, because of the poor performance by the students tested, the state Board of Education reduced the cut-point for passing to 55 percent. Students will also get to take the HSEE multiple times if they fail to achieve a passing score.

Ever present in the background of the accountability law are California's academic content standards. The state's standards are among the best in the nation. In its 2000 survey of state standards, the Thomas B. Fordham Foundation ranked California's standards for English, mathematics, history, and science as number one in the country or tied for number one.[16] California's standards are rigorous, specific, comprehensive, and cumulative.

Given this description of California's accountability system, what can we say about how well the system addresses the Goertz criteria set forth at the beginning of this chapter? First, what are schools accountable for? Under California's system, this has so far been unclear. Because the Stanford-9 is not aligned with the state academic content standards, it is uncertain whether schools should be accountable for the material tested on Stanford-9 or the content contained in the standards. Also, when the California legislature enacted the state's accountability law in 1999, it said that the Academic Performance Index was to include such nontest measures as graduation rates and student and teacher attendance rates. For the time being,

---

[16]See "The State of State Standards 2000," Chester Finn and Michael J. Petrilli, editors, The Thomas B. Fordham Foundation, Washington, DC, January 2000.

though, the state has excluded these nontest measures when it calculates the index. Governor Davis has, in fact, turned down recommendations from the state superintendent of public instruction to include them. The Davis administration is supposed to conduct a study that will help set a timetable for including these measures in the Academic Performance Index calculation. Such uncertainty makes it difficult for schools to determine if they will be held accountable for these measures or not.

For whom are schools accountable? The California system is clear on this point. All students, with the exception of a small number of students with individual education plans that exempt them from testing and students with parents or guardians who request an exemption, must take the Stanford-9, including students who do not speak English. Spanish-speaking students who do not speak English and have been in the California school system for less than twelve months must take both the Stanford-9 and an additional test in Spanish. Some renegade school districts in California, however, such as San Francisco Unified, have refused to test large numbers of non-English-speaking students. In those districts, it is less clear for whom the schools are accountable.

Is progress measured absolutely or relatively? In California, the state government measures the progress of schools relatively through annual growth targets for test scores. As mentioned earlier, little growth is called for, and it will take years for many schools to reach the state-recommended Academic Performance Index performance target of 800 even if they meet their annual growth goals.

Is the accountability system fair? Although California's accountability system is based to a large extent on aggregate test scores, the state also requires that various subgroups, including ethnic minorities and the socioeconomically disadvantaged, improve their performance. With this requirement, it is less likely that improvement efforts will ignore some group of students.

However, because California's rewards and sanctions program is voluntary, children are trapped in poor-performing schools that refuse to participate in the state program. Such a situation is not fair to the students in these failing schools and to the schools that recognize their deficiencies and actually try to improve.

Is the accountability system informative? The answer is yes and no. Local districts report individual test scores to parents. However, for the general public, the state reports scores and rankings on a school-by-school basis using schoolwide averages. No one reports individual student scores longitudinally, so it is impossible to tell which teachers are effective and which are ineffective in improving student achievement. Also, many school districts are not able to track student achievement from one year to the next, with the result that a teacher may have no prior-year testing information about students. Further, even in districts with well-integrated information systems, the district may receive no testing information for students coming from another district. Now the state is in the process of establishing an Academic Performance Index database that will include longitudinal data on individual student test scores. This database could be used in the future for a value-added analysis showing how much individual students improve their performance each year. This database could also allow districts to provide information on test results to teachers and (in the case of transfer students) to other districts.[17]

In addition to the Goertz criteria, there are several other key questions. For instance, under California's accountability system, how much are assessment and classroom instruction aligned with the state standards? As noted, although California has an extraordinarily good set of standards, there have been major alignment problems with the accountability system. The state Legislative

---

[17]See Legislative Analyst's Office, op. cit., E-127.

Analyst's Office aptly points out the dilemma created by nonalignment:

> Since the Stanford-9 tests a different set of information than the content standards, the state is sending conflicting messages about what schools should be teaching. Should teachers and administrators focus instruction on areas covered by the Stanford-9? The state is offering bonuses that can exceed $25,000 per individual for success measured by that test. Or should they teach what is expected under the academic content standards for which the state has invested $1 billion for new textbooks, the Governor is proposing $335 million for staff development, and upon which the [High School Exit Exam] is based?[18]

California, however, is in the process of making a transition to standards-aligned assessment. The state Legislative Analyst's Office says that, assuming there are no problems with the validity of the grading standards or the tests themselves, it would be feasible to include results from the standards-based tests in the Academic Performance Index for 2002.[19] Once a standards-aligned assessment is officially part of the accountability system, there will be greater incentive to teach to the standards as opposed to teaching to a nonstandards-aligned test (the Stanford-9). Given the high quality of California's standards, such a development should help improve learning in the classroom and increase true student achievement. The state also will be trying to help teachers by spending a significant amount of money on training already-hired teachers to teach the material in the state standards.

Finally, do the rewards and sanctions in California's accountability system give students, teachers, and administrators real incentives to improve? For some schools perhaps, but for many others the answer is no. The incremental growth targets for low-performing schools are quite small.[20] Also, participation in the intervention program is voluntary,

---

[18]Legislative Analyst's Office, op., E-92.

[19]Ibid., E-96.

[20]For schools scoring above the state-recommended API target of 800, the annual growth target is a single point. Ibid., E-94.

and even those that apply may be turned down in the state selection process. Thus, the lowest performing schools in the state may not be participating in the intervention program and therefore remain beyond the reach of the state's improvement efforts and sanctions. Further, if the lowest performing school in the state meets its minimal growth target, it is ineligible to apply for assistance under this program. Because the intervention program is voluntary and selective, out of the more than 3,100 schools in California that fall below the fiftieth percentile on the Stanford-9, only 830 are participating in the program.

There are other significant omissions from the California system that dilute the incentive to improve. Unlike Florida, students attending a failing California school are not eligible for a state-funded exit voucher to attend a private school. This lack of a parental choice mechanism can trap students, especially students from poor households, in a failing public school. Without having to worry about the potential loss of their customer base, public school officials have less incentive to improve student achievement.

Also, under the 1999 accountability law, there is little incentive for students to do their best on the accountability tests. Sanctions do not fall on them if they fail to perform their best on the tests, although a bill passed in 2000 does allot increased funds for students who do well on the standards test. Some commentators say that high school student scores on the tests are as low as they are because high school students give only a token effort when taking the tests, since they suffer no repercussions for such half-hearted behavior. This is not the case with the HSEE, where students may not receive their high school diplomas if they fail to pass the exam.

As for teachers, the state rewards them with bonuses if they work at schools where students perform exceptionally better than before. However, in the accountability system, rewards and sanctions are not tied to individual teacher performance. Poor teaching by an individual teacher does not automatically invite any sanction. Yet recent research shows that teacher quality and effectiveness is perhaps the most important factor in determining student achievement. The lack of a nexus in the California accountability system between individual teacher performance and student performance on state assessments constitutes a huge hole in the accountability system.

It should also be noted that the state's schools of education, which prepare and produce California's teachers, are also absent from the accountability system. If too many teachers in California are not performing well, the state's schools of education must bear some of the responsibility. Yet they are left completely out of the accountability equation.

Ultimately, it is up to the discretion of the elected state superintendent of public instruction to use many sanctions available under California's accountability system. Political concerns clearly play a role in this process. Over the last several decades, the state teachers unions have been strong allies of the state superintendents. Given the unions' antipathy to charter schools and renegotiation of collective bargaining contracts, it is difficult to imagine a union-allied superintendent using many of the discretionary powers allocated under the 1999 accountability law. Thus, many sanctions may end up as mere paper tigers, depending on who is occupying the superintendent's office. Such a situation, again, argues in favor of a sanction, such as Florida's exit-voucher option, which places sanction power in the hands of parents rather than a politician.

As of fall 2001, the state had not imposed sanctions on any school in California because low-performing schools in the accountability program were in the second year of the two-year period in which they had to show improvement.[21] The State Legislature was still in the process of determining what types of warnings the state would give to nonimproving low-performing schools and when it would deliver those warnings.

Under the California system, principals, superintendents, and school boards are held to some accountability. Princi-

---

[21]The authors benefited from discussions with Roger Magyar on the material in this paragaph.

pals may be reassigned, and the state can take over schools. However, if no one holds teachers individually accountable for their effectiveness, is it fair to hold principals and school boards accountable? Is it fair to hold a principal accountable for student performance at his or her school if he or she cannot hold individual teachers at the school accountable for their performance?

The sanctions portion of the California system, thus, is porous and inadequate. Add on the other deficiencies in the system and we must conclude that not only is accountability in California a work in progress, but it also still needs work.

TEXAS

Texas' business leaders were worried about the quality of the state's workforce and wanted more accountability in the schools. They worked with politicians and parents to promote school reform. The state began by creating its own tests and then started to rate schools based on their test scores. This rating and accountability system has led to gains in student learning.

In 1993, the Texas Legislature passed statutes that mandated the creation of the Texas public school accountability system to accredit school districts and rate schools. The foundation of the Texas accountability system has been the state test, the Texas Assessment of Academic Skills (TAAS), first implemented in 1990. The major parts of the accountability system, including student accountability, school accountability, the performance database, the accountability rating system, and the rewards and sanctions program, are all based to a great extent on TAAS results.

The TAAS exam tests reading and math in grades 3–8, writing in grades 4 and 8, and science and social studies in grade 8. Also, there are exit examinations in reading, mathematics, and writing in grade 10 and end-of-course examinations in English, U.S. history, biology, and Algebra I. Whereas

California has used the norm-referenced Stanford-9, TAAS is not a norm-referenced test. It is a criterion-referenced exam that is designed to measure competency on Texas' statewide curriculum. The curriculum was first implemented in 1985 and later updated by the Texas Board of Education in 1997. The state department of education has produced "educator guides" that are designed to show what components of the curriculum may be tested on the TAAS.

TAAS tests all students, rather than a sample, and uses largely multiple-choice questions. The TAAS writing assessments in grades 4, 8, and 10 include short-answer questions and essays.

It is widely believed that students must answer correctly 70 percent of all items on a TAAS test in order to pass. The reality, however, is much more complicated. Although the Texas Board of Education in 1990 adopted a 70 percent standard for passing/minimum expectations in writing, reading, and mathematics, the state department of education says that, "The passing standards for the TAAS and the end-of-course tests are related to two factors: 1) the difficulty of the items on the tests and 2) the number of the items students have to answer correctly to pass."[22] Because test items fluctuate in difficulty from year to year, the state department explains that the performance standard for passing is adjusted:

> For instance, suppose a test contains fairly easy items when a standard is set at 70%. A subsequent test is administered with slightly more difficult items. If the standard of 70% of the items on the test were used exclusively, the students taking the second test would be held to a higher standard than the students taking the first test. The percent of items required to pass would be the same, but the difficulty of the items would not be. In order to set the standard on the second test to an achievement level equivalent to that of the first test, the tests are equated, and the percent required to pass is adjusted. In this case, the percent of

---

[22]"Texas Student Assessment Program Technical Digest of the Academic Year 1999–2000," Texas Education Agency, NCS Pearson, Harcourt Educational Measurement Inc., and BETA, Inc., 2001: 36.

the items required to pass the second test would be less than 70%, since the items were more difficult.[23]

Because Texas is implementing a new set of academic content standards, the more rigorous Texas Essential Knowledge and Skills (TEKS), more difficult questions have been added to the TAAS exams in recent years. Thus, in an extreme example of passing-score adjustment, on the 2001 sixth grade TAAS math test, a student had to answer correctly only twenty-eight out of fifty-six questions, or only 50 percent, in order to pass the exam. In 1998 and 1999, a sixth grader would have had to answer correctly thirty-eight out of fifty-six questions in order to pass.[24]

Texas education officials defend the scoring adjustment process by saying that it is needed in order to compare current score results with results from previous years. However, there is a problem with this logic: If students in Texas are now expected to master the material in a new set of academic content standards (namely, TEKS) that is supposed to be more rigorous, then state education officials must believe that students should be performing at a higher level than was previously expected of them. To adjust passing scores downward in order to compensate for the increased difficulty of the academic content standards contradicts the purpose of the new standards, which is to raise the level of student performance.

Further, because the percentage of students passing the TAAS, 82 percent, rose again in 2001, the fourth increase in a row, testing experts cast doubt on the scoring adjustment process. Walter Haney of the Center for the Study of Testing, Evaluation, and Education Policy at Boston College says, "The lower minimum scores to pass [math] could be a factor in the increased percentage of students who passed the TAAS this year."[25] Haney also noted that passing rates

---

[23]Ibid.

[24]"Bar for Passing TAAS Lowered," *Dallas Morning News*, June 9, 2001, available at <http://www.dallasnews.com/cgi-bin/print/cgi?story=.../389136_taaspassing_09.htm>.

[25]Ibid.

typically drop, not increase, when tougher test items are introduced.[26]

The Texas accountability system has several key components. First, there is the school report card that all schools must compile and give to each parent. The state department of education (called the Texas Education Agency) created the requirements for the school report cards. Cards must include a school's TAAS passing rates by ethnic and socioeconomic subgroup; the average TAAS passing rates for state, district, and school; and test-taking exemptions for regular, non-English-speaking, and learning-disabled students by subject for ethnic and socioeconomic subgroups. In addition, the school report card must include information on attendance and dropout rates, end-of-course exam participation, the student-teacher ratio, the completion rate for the Recommended High School Program, and administrative and instructional costs per pupil.

Although the school report cards are supposed to put pressure on schools to do well by keeping parents informed, the Texas system also contains more concrete measures to hold students and schools accountable. Students must pass the four high school end-of-course exams or the exit exam in order to graduate. Schools are subject to various rewards and sanctions (which will be discussed later in this section) based on TAAS scores.

Texas has also devised an accountability rating system that uses TAAS performance (without the end-of-course exam results), dropout rate, and attendance rate to calculate annual progress for schools and districts. The state has rated schools and districts since 1994. The rating system has four performance levels:[27]

---

   [26]Ibid.

   [27]Margaret E. Goertz, Mark C. Duffy, and Kerstin Carlson-Le Floch, "Assessment and Accountability Systems in the 50 States: 1999–2000—Assessment and Accountability Systems: 50 State Profiles," Consortium for Public Policy Research in Education, University of Pennsylvania Graduate School of Education, March 2001 (CPRE Report Series RR–046), <http://www.gse.upenn.edu/cpre/Publications/Publications_Accountability.htm: TX 3-4>.

1. Exemplary (90 percent of total students and each ethnic and socioeconomic subgroup passing each subject, a dropout rate of 1 percent or less for all students and subgroups, and an attendance rate of 94 percent or higher)

2. Recognized (at least 80 percent of total students and each subgroup passing each subject, a dropout rate of 3.5 percent or less for all students and subgroups, and an attendance rate of 94 percent or higher)

3. Academically Acceptable/Acceptable (at least 50 percent of total students and each subgroup passing each subject, a dropout rate of 6 percent or less for all students and subgroups, and an attendance rate of 94 percent or higher)

4. Unacceptable/Low-Performing (below 50 percent of total students and each subgroup passing each subject, a dropout rate of above 6 percent for all students and subgroups, and an attendance rate below 94 percent)

The state determines that a school or a district has made adequate yearly progress if it achieves an "acceptable" rating.[28] In addition, a district cannot be rated Exemplary or Recognized if it has one or more Low-Performing schools or has 1,000 or more, or 10 percent or more, students in grades 7–12 who were unreported on either the comprehensive student-level information system enrollment record or the school dropout record.

In order to calculate the information necessary for the accountability rating system and for other elements of the general accountability system, Texas combines demographic information and performance data in its Academic Excellence Indicator System. The Indicator System brings together:

1. TAAS passing rate
   - by grade
   - by subject

---

[28]Ibid., TX 4.

- by all grades
- by subgroup

2. End-of-course exam passing rates

3. Annual attendance rates

4. Annual dropout rates

5. High school graduation rates

6. Percent of high school students completing an advanced course

7. Percent of high school graduates completing the Recommended High School Program

8. Advanced Placement and International Baccalaureate results

9. SAT and ACT participation and results[29]

Like California's Similar Schools Index, Texas uses a statistical tool (called Comparable Improvement) to compare schools with similar characteristics and to measure school-level growth. Under Comparative Improvement, a school is compared with a forty-school group that shares similar ethnic, socioeconomic, student mobility, and non-English-speaking characteristics. Comparative Improvement is based on the Texas Learning Index, which uses TAAS reading and math in grades 3–8 and in exit exams. Texas Learning Index growth scores are calculated using student Texas Learning Index growth (an individual student's current-year score in math and reading minus the student's prior-year score) and campus average Texas Learning Index growth (sum of student Texas Learning Index growth by subject divided by the total number of students by subject). Schools are ranked in quartiles based on Texas Learning Index growth. Also calculated are the number of students at each school meeting or exceeding the Texas Learning Index growth standard and the number of

---

[29]Ibid., TX 3.

students performing at high or low levels. The state distributes a Comparative Improvement report with each school's Indicator System report.

Once the state makes all these various ratings and calculations, the state bestows a variety of rewards and sanctions on schools. If a school has an Exemplary, Recognized, or even Acceptable rating, it is eligible to participate in a rewards program called the Texas Successful Schools Award System. The state awards school bonuses of between $500 and $5,000 if a school's Comparative Improvement quartile ranking, based on Texas Learning Index average growth, puts the school in the top quartile of the forty-school comparison group in reading and math.

At the other end of the spectrum, a Low-Performing school is subject to a number of interventions and sanctions, including having the local school board hold a public hearing, submitting an improvement plan to the state, holding a state hearing, appointing a special on-site intervention team, appointing a board of managers from district residents, or closing the school down. If the state appoints a special intervention team, the team evaluates the school to determine the cause of poor performance, recommends remedies, assists in developing a school-improvement plan, and helps monitor the school.

Few schools, however, ever receive the harsher sanctions available to state officials.[30] For example, the state commissioner of education can send monitors, with limited authority, into schools to make suggestions of remedies to the local school superintendent. If a school makes inadequate progress after the appointment of a monitor, the state sends in a master, who has full authority over the local school board and superintendent. Currently, there are seven schools in Texas under the supervision of a monitor and two under the supervision of a master.

---

[30]The authors have benefited from discussions with Chris Patterson on this topic.

In addition, although the state may reconstitute a failing school (an entire staff may be transferred and a new one brought in) or close it down, only a handful of schools have ever been subject to these sanctions. Indeed, the state has reconstituted only three schools, all in the San Antonio Independent School District, under the Texas accountability program. The state commissioner may also put failing schools under an outside management board. Such an action, considered a severe penalty, has only occurred once in Texas.

For low-performing districts, the state education commissioner may also conduct a Special Accreditation Investigation to examine situations identified through complaints, low performance ratings, or state-initiated analyses. Specifically, an accreditation investigation can be initiated if there are severe problems in governance, finances, testing practices, data quality, education of the learning-disabled, compliance with federal regulation, or administrative management. If the results of an accreditation investigation indicate that the state should impose sanctions, the commissioner may take away the district's accreditation, lower the district's accountability rating, or both.

Texas does not hand out special grants or additional resources to Low-Performing schools, although state regional education service centers can contact a district about various services available to such schools. Assistance to Low-Performing schools includes data analysis, identification of problems, information about effective practices, and curriculum alignment.

The accountability system not only provides information to parents about which schools are performing poorly, but it also provides some relief to parents whose children are attending Low-Performing schools. As part of the accountability program, in 1995, the Texas legislature created the Public Education Grant Program that permits parents with children attending a Low-Performing school to transfer to another public school, even one outside district boundaries, that had higher performance results.

Under the Texas accountability system, what are schools accountable for? The simple answer is: The accountability rating system makes schools accountable for test scores, dropout rates, and attendance rates. However, because so much of the state's accountability system relies on the TAAS, the real and more complex question is: What does the TAAS hold schools accountable for? It is this question that has stirred up a hornet's nest of controversy in Texas.

Over the years, the passing rate on the TAAS has increased substantially. In 2000, the percentage of students passing the reading, math, and writing sections of the TAAS exams in grades 3–8 and grade 10 was 80 percent, up from 56 percent in 1994. Poor and minority students made the highest gains. Passing all sections of the tenth grade TAAS exit exam is a requirement for graduation. In 2000, 80 percent of tenth grade students taking the tenth grade exam passed all sections, up from 50 percent in 1994. If they fail to pass the tenth grade TAAS, students have eight chances to pass it again. Among students who took the exit exam in 1998 and who were in the same school district in 2000, 92 percent had passed the test.[31] For all these gains, though, the question is whether these increases in passing rates represent real increases in learning.

For those who argue that TAAS score increases do not represent improved learning, the biggest complaint against the TAAS exam centers on its lack of rigor. Jeff Judson, president of the Texas Public Policy Foundation, notes that the TAAS is a minimum proficiency test, not an achievement test, and, therefore, "A perfect score means the student has met minimum expectations."[32] Judson observes that because a student

---

[31]Craig D. Jerald, "Real Results, Remaining Challenges: The Story of Texas Education Reform," The Business Roundtable and The Education Trust, April 2001: 11–12.

[32]Jeff Judson, "A Review of the Texas Public School Accountability System," Veritas, Winter 2001: 34.

can get 30 percent of TAAS questions wrong and still pass the exam, "students are passing the test even though they are only able to answer questions that are one, two, or three years below grade level."[33] Indeed, a team from Mathematically Correct found that from 1995 to 1998, questions on the fifth grade TAAS exam, for example, could be written at the third, fourth, or fifth grade level (as outlined in Texas' state standards). Questions, therefore, averaged approximately one year below the grade level being tested.[34] Many observers say that, at best, the tenth grade TAAS exit exams measure only eighth grade–level knowledge and skills.[35] One analysis found that achievement at the sixth grade level, as measured by the California math standards, was sufficient to pass the TAAS exit exam.[36]

In its recent analysis of TAAS scores, the Dallas school district found that passing the TAAS reading exam in grades 3–8 was equivalent to performing only at the twenty-fifth percentile on the Iowa Test of Basic Skills (ITBS). Passing the TAAS math exam in grades 3–5 was equivalent to the fortieth percentile on the ITBS, whereas passing the TAAS math exam in grades 6–8 was equivalent to the thirty-third percentile on ITBS.[37]

Others defend the TAAS exams, saying that the rising TAAS scores are matched by improved student performance on other tests, such as the National Assessment of Educational Progress (NAEP). For example, on the 1996 NAEP fourth grade math exam, Texas ranked among the top states, and its students tied for the greatest increase in scores from 1992 to 1996. Also on that test, Texas African American and Latino students outscored students from the same groups in

---

[33]Ibid.

[34]Paul Clopton, "Texas Mathematics Education in Transition," *Texas Education Review,* Fall 2000: 57.

[35]Craig D. Jerald, op. cit., 7.

[36]Paul Clopton, op. cit., 57.

[37]Dallas Public Schools Education Committee, "TEA Position on Using TAAS Data and TAAS-Norm-Referenced Comparisons," Dallas, TX, February 9, 1999: 1.

virtually every other state. On the 1998 eighth grade NAEP writing exam, the percentage of Texas Latino students scoring at the NAEP's "proficient" level was twice the national average, while the percentage of African American students scoring at the "proficient" level was nearly three times the national average.[38] A Business Roundtable-Education Trust report calculated that if African American fourth graders in every state scored as well in math as those in Texas, the national achievement gap between white and African American fourth graders in math would close by a third. The report also calculated that if African American eighth graders everywhere wrote as well as their peers in Texas, the national achievement gap between white and African-American eighth graders in writing would be cut in half.[39]

Two well-publicized Rand Corporation reports have offered seemingly contradictory conclusions on the TAAS and the NAEP. A June 2000 Rand report found that states like Texas that had extensive accountability systems had the highest and most improved NAEP scores. That report said that the TAAS was an important factor in improving NAEP-measured academic achievement.[40] An October 2000 Rand report, however, questioned the validity of TAAS scores by showing that those scores did not correlate with the results of other standardized tests. Also, in the 1990s, Texas students' TAAS scores increased more than their NAEP scores.[41]

Harvard researcher Jay P. Greene points out that "It is possible that TAAS, which is based on the mandated Texas curriculum, tests different skills than those tested by the

---

[38]Craig D. Jerald, op. cit., 17.

[39]Ibid., 18.

[40]See David W. Grissmer, Ann Flanagan, Jennifer Kawata, and Stephanie Williamson, "Improving Student Achievement: What NAEP State Test Scores Tell Us," The Rand Corporation, June 25, 2000: 55, 99–100.

[41]See Stephen P. Klein, Laura S. Hamilton, Daniel F. McCaffrey, and Brian M. Stecher, "What Do Test Scores in Texas Tell Us?" Rand Education Issue Paper, October 2000.

national standardized tests. Both could produce valid results and be weakly correlated to each other if they are testing different things."[42] Hoover Institution education economist Eric Hanushek notes that both Rand studies were based on poor research designs and that "neither holds up to a modicum of scrutiny."[43] Greene, who contends that Texas has in reality made remarkable education gains, nonetheless observes that there is "some ambiguity" regarding any conclusions that can be drawn from a comparison of NAEP and TAAS results.[44]

The controversy over the relationship between TAAS and NAEP scores aside, serious questions concerning the role and effect of TAAS in the Texas system still remain. Given the fact that TAAS assesses achievement at low levels, does TAAS put optimal pressure on schools to substantially improve achievement and learning? An analysis of the TAAS math exams by a team of mathematicians and statisticians associated with the math advocacy group Mathematically Correct concluded that "Low-level objectives are unlikely to bring student achievement up to the level of our international competition."[45] Further, the study says

> If the TAAS assessment levels are lower than optimal and there is a focus on minimum achievement relative to those assessments, there is an inherent risk that curriculum and instruction will be swayed toward sub-optimal levels as a result of the assessment process. Thus, it is possible that the TAAS exam system is not nearly as effective as it might be in promoting greater mathematics achievement statewide in Texas.[46]

---

[42]Jay P. Greene, "An Evaluation of the Florida A-Plus Accountability and School Choice Program," Florida State University/Center for Civic Innovation at the Manhattan Institute/Program on Education Policy and Governance, Harvard University, February 2001: 3 (quotation edited to remove an unnecessary comma).

[43]Eric A Hanushek, "Rand versus Rand: The Sequel," *Education Matters,* Spring 2001: 69.

[44]Jay P. Greene, op. cit., 3.

[45]Paul Clopton, Wayne Bishop, and David Klein, "Statewide Mathematics Assessment in Texas," <http://www.mathematicallycorrect.com/lonestar.htm>, 29.

[46]Ibid., 20.

The analysis concludes that the emphasis on minimum achievement on TAAS results in a flawed accountability system:

> [T]he system of mathematics achievement assessment in Texas emerges as a powerful model but one that is too highly focused on minimal achievement. The incentives for improvement that accompany the statewide assessment system do not emphasize high achievement sufficiently. In fact, the design of the assessment devices themselves doesn't even permit the measurement of high achievement levels with any degree of accuracy. Without a substantial adjustment to the objectives that are evidenced by the exam items themselves, it seems unlikely that the assessment system will effectively promote the kind of achievement necessary for students to realize the full benefit of a rigorous mathematics education.[47]

A 2000 study prepared by Laurence A. Toenjes and Jean E. Garst for the state department of education supports the conclusion of the Mathematically Correct group. Though not indicting the entire TAAS-based accountability system, the Toenjes-Garst study notes that "a great many students who do well on the TAAS later do poorly on the Algebra I End-of-Course test."[48] Thus, for example, "of eighth-graders who earned a Texas Learning Index (TLI) score of 80 on the math portion of the TAAS only about 27 percent passed the end-of-course algebra test later as ninth graders."[49]

---

[47]Ibid., 31.

[48]Laurence A. Toenjes and Jean E. Garst, "Identifying High Performing Texas Schools and School Districts and their Methods of Success," prepared for the Texas Education Agency, December 2000: i.

[49]Ibid. Clopton points out: "Although the Algebra 1 [EOC] exam appeared to be at a notably low difficulty level, the jump in grade level achievement required between the 8th- or 10th-grade exams and the Algebra exam was striking, roughly two grade levels by California standards. This suggests that the preparation for algebra, as measured by TAAS exams, is likely to be insufficient, leaving students who pass their TAAS exams at a risk of failure in algebra. . . . Performance criteria in the grades leading up to algebra are simply not sufficient to support success." See Clopton, op. cit., 57–58.

Thus, although increased learning is taking place in Texas, the incentives and pressures created by TAAS may not be promoting as large an improvement as possible.

The TAAS exams have also suffered from changing difficulty levels from year to year. Harvard researcher and standards expert Sandra Stotsky found that "The 1995 [reading TAAS] tests are longer and more difficult than the 1998 tests at all grade levels."[50] Stotsky concludes that "If the scores students achieved on the 1998 tests were higher than those achieved by their counterparts on the 1995 tests, the decline in the overall level of reading difficulty of the selections on these tests . . . suggests that there may have been no real improvement in their reading skills."[51] Indeed, Stotsky says that "There may have even been a decline."[52]

Because the TAAS exams are criterion-referenced, they are supposed to be aligned to the state's standards and curriculum. The Texas academic content standards have received generally good reviews from evaluators. The Thomas B. Fordham Foundation gives the state's standards an overall grade of B, with specific grades of B for the English and math standards.[53] The current standards, the Texas Essential Knowledge and Skills (TEKS), replaced the old Texas Essential Elements in 1998–99. The new standards, evaluators say, are more rigorous than the old, so a test based on new ones should be more challenging than an exam based on the old ones. The state is creating a new TAAS exam, dubbed TAKS, aligned to the new standards, and it will be used in 2003. (In 2004, a new TAAS eleventh grade exit exam will replace the current tenth grade exam. It will cover not only language arts and math but also several other core subjects.)

Skeptics point out, however, that as the test becomes more rigorous, Texas' performance criteria will require lower

---

[50]Sandra Stotsky, "Analysis of the Texas Reading Tests, Grades 4, 8, and 10, 1995–1998," unpublished paper, 1998: 8.
[51]Ibid.
[52]Ibid.
[53]"The State of Standards 2000," op. cit., 115.

cut-scores for passing, which will mean that "the utility of this increase in rigor for stimulating greater achievement is questionable."[54] Further, an independent review of the proposed TAKS, done in cooperation with the state department of education, found that the new TAKS objectives were poorly delineated, were repetitious from grade to grade (with no increase in difficulty from grade to grade), did not reflect the expectations set forth in the new state standards, lacked academic rigor, and covered too few topics too superficially.[55]

For whom are schools accountable in Texas? Originally, only regular education students had to take the TAAS exams. In 1999, the state administered the exam to learning-disabled students and non-English-speaking students (the latter taking the TAAS in a Spanish-language version in various grades). Still, many students receive exemptions from taking the test. In 2000, 13 percent of African American students, 12 percent of Hispanic students, and 14 percent of economically disadvantaged students were not tested, versus 7 percent of whites.[56] Either schools labeled these students learning-disabled or non-English-speaking, or the students were absent, or their school had some other reason for not testing these students. It should be noted that, since 1991, enrollment of the learning-disabled in Texas has increased by 32 percent, with much of that increase consisting of minority students. As Judson points out, those who have fallen outside the

---

[54]Paul Clopton, op. cit., 59. Clopton cites the example of the Algebra 1 TEKS: "The limitations of the TEKS with respect to quadratics are consistent with those throughout the Algebra 1 TEKS. Algebraic methods are de-emphasized, especially when difficult. They are also unnecessarily vague, making students, teachers, and test-designers unsure as to the exact expectations. These characteristics may make higher test scores possible, but they will not promote greater achievement in algebra." Ibid., 61. Clopton concludes that "the shift to a TEKS-based TAAS can provide only a slight improvement at best." Ibid., 59.

[55]See Chris Patterson, testimony to Texas Board of Education, Texas Public Policy Foundation, July 12, 2001.

[56]Craig D. Jerald, op.cit., 10.

accountability system are "ironically the students who most need accountability from the system."[57]

The ease with which schools can meet the performance standard needed to achieve an Acceptable rating in the Texas system has perverse consequences. Because only 50 percent of students at a school have to pass the TAAS in order for the school to gain Acceptable status, schools often focus reduced attention on students who are likely to pass the TAAS and give additional attention only to students who are less likely to pass the exam.[58] Given the fact that the TAAS is not as difficult or rigorous as other tests, many students who can pass TAAS, but not other tests, may not receive as much attention as they should be getting.

Is progress measured absolutely or relatively? In Texas, accountability ratings are based on absolute measures of the percentage of students passing TAAS exams, dropout rates, and attendance rates. Progress is measured through the use of the student growth-based Comparable Improvement indicator.

Is Texas' accountability system fair? Texas law requires that TAAS scores be reported separately for African American, Latino, white, and low-socioeconomic students. The Texas accountability system then requires that in order to achieve a given rating level (e.g., Exemplary, Recognized, etc.), not only must a school meet the test-score target, but all subgroups of students must also meet that target. Thus, for example, to achieve an Acceptable rating, at least 50 percent of all students at a school must pass the TAAS and at least 50 percent of each subgroup of students at the school must also pass the TAAS. No group of students, therefore, can be ignored under the Texas system.

The gap between the passing rates for white and minority TAAS test-takers has decreased significantly from 1994 to 2000. For instance, on the tenth grade exit exam, the gap between whites and African Americans has closed from 36

---

[57]Jeff Judson, op. cit., 34.
[58]Ibid., 33.

percent in 1994 to 22 percent in 2000. On the same exam, the gap between whites and Latinos has closed from 30 percent in 1994 to 19 percent in 2000.

Caution should be used in interpreting these improvements in minority passing rates. If the TAAS is not as difficult as it should be and if state officials have reduced the performance level needed in order to pass the TAAS, then one could expect less room for whites to improve on the test, since they started at a relatively high achievement level. At the same time, minorities, since they started at a lower achievement level, would have more room to improve. When whites improve modestly and minorities improve greatly, this result may seem impressive. But the narrowing of the gap in achievement scores may (or may not) have more to do with the difficulty of the test and how it is scored than with a narrowing of the gap in actual achievement.

Is the Texas accountability system informative? As in the case of California, the answer is yes and no. The state makes available (to parents and the public) school report cards containing TAAS passing rate information, attendance and dropout rates, plus an array of other information. However, the state does not make generally available the longitudinal data on student achievement that would make it possible to evaluate the effectiveness of individual teachers based on value-added calculations.

What about Texas' rewards-and-sanctions program? The various rewards and sanctions have increased pressure on schools and districts to improve their accountability ratings. A study (sponsored by the state department of education) surveyed school and district administrators and found a great deal of pressure to improve. One local superintendent said that his district allows new principals three years to move their school up to a Recognized rating level. For principals of schools that have been awarded a Recognized rating but then slide back below Recognized in a given year, this district gives the principal one year to return the school to its previous Recognized status. In another district, principals are told that if their school is not at the Recognized level by the close of the school year, they should not anticipate a renewal of their contract.[59]

Further, the study sponsored by the state department of education found that all middle schools and high schools surveyed had teams working to align the math curriculum with the new Texas standards. What schools were doing varied from school to school. Some schools held general discussions, whereas others made an in-depth effort to coordinate curriculum designs.[60]

There are problems, though. When researchers for this study asked whether districts had a continuous TAAS-based cycle of teaching, testing, data analysis, and reteaching, they found enormous variability across districts.[61]

Also, programs designed to assist low-performing students have serious irregularities. First, the criteria for determining exactly which students are considered low-performing differed markedly from school to school. For example, schools varied in criteria they used to categorize students as low-performing in mathematics. The Toenjes study cites criteria from five separate campuses:

1. Only students who failed the TAAS math test

2. Students who failed TAAS together with students failing a math class

3. Students who scored low on a standardized pretest, such as the ITBS, together with those who also failed TAAS

4. Only students who fail a math class during the year

5. Only students who are recommended by teachers[62]

---

[59]Laurence A. Toenjes and Jean E. Garst, op. cit., 28.
[60]Ibid., 30.
[61]Ibid., 40.
[62]Ibid., 34.

Thus, a student considered low-performing at one school is not considered low-performing at another (and is therefore not eligible for special assistance). Further, the study found inconsistency in record-keeping from school to school. Some schools closely watch the scores of low-performing students, whereas at other schools there is no focus whatsoever on the ongoing performance of these students.[63]

Local school administrators also said that rules and constraints imposed by electives and sports made it impossible to have mandatory programs for low-performing students in math. Although all the districts surveyed do provide programs that students can sign up for to get help in math, many of the programs are offered for only part of the year (usually the second semester in preparation for the spring TAAS).[64] Of course, this means that many students end up not getting assistance either because they decide not to take advantage of the voluntary program or because the program is not offered at a particular time of the year. Even where low-performing students voluntarily attend after-school or tutoring classes, the study found that "usually no single teacher or administrator has responsibility for monitoring their progress to see if any real gains are being made."[65] Indeed, schools simply go through the motions in their remedial activity. The result is: "Whether or not the student actually is making progress is not discovered until the next TAAS testing. Therefore, many low-performers become chronic failures."[66]

Students do have an incentive to do well enough on the tenth grade TAAS exit exam to earn their high school diploma. However, rather little happens to students who don't do well on other TAAS tests.

As for teachers, the state accountability system does not formally tie rewards or sanctions to individual teacher

---

[63]Ibid.
[64]Ibid.
[65]Ibid.
[66]Ibid.

performance. But in a right-to-work state with union rules that are less encumbering than those in other states, local school officials may have more freedom to address individual teacher performance. (For this, it would be helpful if the state made value-added data generally available.) Also, as previously noted, many districts are willing to fire principals who do not improve their school's accountability rating.

Although the state allows students attending a poor-performing school to transfer to a better-performing public school, the state does not tell districts to fund exit vouchers for such students to attend private schools, nor does the state fund such vouchers itself. In the absence of exit vouchers, students from poor households are likely to remain in the public school system in comparatively weak schools. Because, in most cases, students cannot use an exit voucher to leave the public system and take funding with them, public school officials have less incentive to improve student achievement.

In sum, there is certainly good news in Texas. Even critics acknowledge that because the state set up its accountability system, students are learning more than they did before. Nonetheless, many problems remain, and the state needs to address them, especially in the area of testing. Texas officials have said from the outset that their system was an evolving one. Time will tell if the final product is worth the growing pains.

FLORIDA

In 1999, Florida enacted the A-Plus accountability program. The program includes a number of unique and innovative features and, as a result, has been widely discussed. Prominent features of the system include a new standards-aligned test, school grading, merit pay for teachers, and exit vouchers for students in failing public schools.

Results from the Florida Comprehensive Assessment Test (FCAT) are the cornerstone of the A-Plus accountability program. The test contains two basic components: a portion measuring selected benchmarks in reading, writing, and mathematics based on the Sunshine State Standards, the state's academic content standards; and, from 2000–01, a second part measuring each student's performance against national norms. Thus, the test contains both criterion-referenced and norm-referenced sections.

Beginning in 2000–2001, FCAT tests grades 3–10 (previously, only grades 4, 8, and 10 were tested in reading and grades 5, 8, and 10 in math). The FCAT reading exam assesses students' ability to construct meaning from informational text and from literature. The FCAT math exam assesses students in six areas, including number sense, concepts and operations, measurement, geometry and spatial sense, algebraic thinking, and data analysis and probability. FCAT includes multiple-choice questions and constructed-response questions (questions where students write an answer, solve a problem, give an explanation, or draw a sketch).

FCAT has five grades (also called performance-standards levels), Levels 1 to 5 (with 5 being the top level). The definitions of the levels are:

• Level 5: The student has success with the most challenging state content standards and answers most of the test questions correctly, including the most challenging ones.

• Level 4: The student has success with the challenging state content standards and answers most of the test questions correctly but may have only some success on the most challenging ones.

• Level 3: The student has partial success with the state standards but performs inconsistently, answering many of the questions correctly but having less success on the most challenging ones.

• Level 2: The student has limited success with the challenging content of the state standards.

- Level 1: The student has little success with the state standards.[67]

Student FCAT scores range between 500 for Level 5 and 100 for Level 1.[68]

In addition to the FCAT, Florida has two other state tests: a writing exam and a high school exit exam. The writing exam, Florida Writes!, is given in grades 4, 8, and 10. The exam is performance-based and criterion-referenced. It has achievement levels ranging from 6.0 (high) to 1.0 (low). In California, students who do poorly on the state-sponsored standardized tests face little in the way of consequences, but in Florida, students must meet standards (as assessed by FCAT and the writing exam) in order to be promoted to the next grade.

The High School Competency Assessment Test (HSCAT) is a criterion-referenced exit exam administered in the eleventh grade. A student must pass the reading, writing, and math sections of HSCAT to receive a high school diploma. Florida is phasing out the HSCAT. Students can currently substitute the tenth grade FCAT for the HSCAT, and by 2003, the HSCAT will be discontinued in favor of the FCAT.

Under the A-Plus plan, the state grades schools on an A–F scale. In December 2001, Gov. Jeb Bush and the Florida cabinet approved changes to the original criteria for the various grades. The new grading system, which state officials believe will slightly increase the number of schools receiving As and Fs, will use a point system based on student performance on the FCAT. Under the new grading formula, a school's performance will be measured in three ways:

- The percentage of students scoring at the highest three levels on the reading, math, and writing tests.

---

[67]Margaret Goertz and Mark Duffy, op. cit., FL 3.
[68]Holly Stepp, "Gov. Bush, Cabinet OK New School-Grading Rule," *Miami Herald,* December 19, 2001, 1B.

• The individual progress made by each student over his or her previous year's FCAT score.

• The improvements in reading scores made by the lowest-performing 25 percent of students.[69]

Specifically, schools will earn points that will determine their grade based upon various student performance indicators:

• One point for each percent of students who score at Level 3 or higher in reading. So, if 25 percent of students at a school score at Level 3 or higher in reading, the school receives twenty-five points.

• One point for each percent of students who score at Level 3 or higher in math.

• One point for each percent of students who score at Level 3 or higher in writing, then averaged with the percent of those who score at Level 3.5 or higher.

• One point for each percent of students who make annual gains in reading.

• One point for each percent of students who make annual gains in math.

• One point for each percent among the lowest 25 percent of students at a school who make annual gains in reading.[70]

After adding up all the points, a school's final grade will be based on the following scale:

• A: At least 410 points
• B: At least 380 points
• C: At least 320 points
• D: At least 280 points
• F: Less than 280 points[71]

---

[69]Ibid.
[70]Ibid.
[71]Ibid.

Under the previous grading system, it was possible for schools to count on their higher performing students to mask the low performance of other students. Florida officials believe that the new grading system, which emphasizes individual student performance, will force schools to address the achievement problems of low-performing students. Gerry Richardson, director of evaluation and reporting for the Florida Department of Education, points out: "If before schools were counting on their highest-achieving students to make up for the ones who were struggling, that is no longer acceptable. Schools will have to make sure that all of their students are making progress."[72] Adds Betty Coxe, deputy commissioner of educational programs: "There shouldn't be a principal or teacher in the state saying, 'Oh, now that the state is going to grade us on whether all our students can read, we'll actually teach them all to read.' It should have been a priority all along."[73] The new grading system's increased focus on individual student performance, therefore, will act as an incentive for schools to improve the achievement of all students.

Florida has not set "passing" scores for any grade level for the FCAT except for grade 10. The state simply reports scores on a scale from 100 to 500 and in terms of the achievement levels (with cut-scores for each level). The state provides FCAT results for each individual student, school, and district, as well as statewide data. The state reports a total score for each student on each test. The state also reports the student's performance on different strands of academic content and in terms of the five achievement levels. In addition, the state reports the student's ranking within Florida itself and as compared to national norms. For schools, districts, and the state overall, the state produces A-Plus reports showing average scores and the percentage of students performing at the five achievement levels.[74]

---

[72]Ibid.

[73]Ibid.

[74]Florida Department of Education, "FCAT Briefing Book," Tallahassee, FL, February 2001: 4, 8.

Florida plans to use the FCAT results for value-added analysis, which will report an individual student's progress from one year to the next. Value-added analysis, which Tennessee uses in its accountability system, provides statistical measures of the influence that school districts, schools, and teachers have on student learning. According to Tennessee education officials, one of the most powerful and controversial aspects of value-added assessment "is that it can reach beyond the school level to produce a measure of an individual teacher's effectiveness, based on how well the students in his or her classroom perform each year."[75] The Florida Department of Education seems to agree, noting, "The progress of all students in a school can be reported in terms of individual teachers who provide instruction to those students."[76] As a consequence, individual teachers can be held accountable for how much they add to the learning of their students.

Florida issues a School Accountability Report that grades each school using the A–F scale. The report also includes the percentage of students scoring at each achievement level within a school, plus a school's suspension rate, absentee rate over twenty days, dropout rate, promotion rate, percent receiving free-or-reduced lunch, and mobility rate.

The A-Plus program provides a number of rewards for schools and teachers. Schools qualify for additional funding if they meet the higher performing grade A criteria, show significant improvement, or improve by one letter grade from one year to the next. The funding is allocated on a per-student basis.

In 1997, the Florida legislature required school boards to base a portion of each employee's compensation on performance. Hence, local superintendents must propose a schedule for teachers' salaries that is based in part on student performance. Local districts decide on these

---

[75]Margaret Goertz and Mark Duffy, op. cit., TN 13.
[76]"FCAT Briefing Book," op. cit., 5.

salary schedules, and the state does not mandate how much of a teacher's salary must be based on the achievement of students. Revisions passed in 1999 require that evaluations of teachers and administrators be based on the performance of students assigned to their classrooms or schools. In other words, local administrators are to judge teachers based on their individual performance in the classroom, not as part of a collective schoolwide body of teachers.

Also in 1999, when the legislature passed A-Plus, it mandated that teachers and administrators who demonstrate outstanding performance (based upon student achievement) could earn annual bonuses of up to 5 percent of their base pay. The bonuses under this unique merit-pay system will be based on FCAT results and will begin in 2002. Some teachers have worried that this legislation could be interpreted as also implying a 5 percent pay cut for teachers at low-performing schools. Governor Jeb Bush, however, in a teleconference with Florida teachers, has repudiated the pay-cut interpretation.[77] Florida's planned value-added FCAT measurement system will be a useful tool in rewarding individual teacher performance through these merit bonuses.

Low-performing schools are subject to a variety of sanctions. A school or district receiving a D or F grade is eligible for the following: (1) state intervention, assistance, and funding; (2) a community assessment team to make recommendations for intervention and assistance to improve the school's performance; (3) priority to receive technical assistance and training services from the state; (4) priority in the use of state supplemental funds; (5) district intervention and assistance; and (6) district authority to declare an emergency and to negotiate special provisions to free the schools from contract restrictions that limit the school's ability to improve student performance.

---

[77]"Bush Defends A-Plus Plan, Says Teacher Bonuses Misunderstood," *Florida Sun-Sentinel*, April 10, 2000.

If a school has received an F grade in any two years of a four-year period, students at that school may: (1) attend a higher performing public school in the district, (2) attend a higher performing public school in an adjacent district as long as there is space available, (3) stay at the same public school, or (4) receive an exit voucher to attend a private (sectarian or nonsectarian) school. We will discuss this latter option, the so-called "voucher sanction," in greater detail below.

For what are Florida schools accountable? The FCAT is a criterion-referenced exam based on the state academic content standards. The Thomas B. Fordham Foundation has given Florida's English-language arts standards a B grade and given a disappointing grade of D to the state's math standards. The Fordham reviewers criticized the math standards for having expectations that "are too often very low indeed."[78] A statewide test based on such standards might, then, also have expectations that are too low.

On the other hand, Greene, in his study of the A-Plus program, found that, unlike TAAS, FCAT stacked up reasonably well against standardized tests like the Stanford-9, which Florida students took under low-stakes circumstances in spring 2000. According to Greene:

> In the second Rand Corporation study of TAAS in Texas, Stephen Klein and his colleagues never found a correlation of more than .21 between the school level results from TAAS and the school level results of low stakes standardized tests. In this analysis, we never found a correlation between FCAT and standardized tests below .86. All of these correlations in Florida are statistically significant, meaning that the strong relationship between the results of the two tests is very unlikely to have been produced by chance.[79]

Greene concluded that such numbers support the validity of the FCAT reading and math scores and that "Schools in

---

[78]"The State of Standards," op. cit., 44.
[79]Jay P. Greene, op. cit., 5–6.

Florida perform on the high stakes FCAT similarly to how they perform on the low stakes Stanford-9."[80]

Greene's findings have to be understood in context. His study is only trying to see if Florida's schools responded to incentives. He wanted to know if, faced with rewards and sanctions, Florida's scores went up or not. One should not assume from his study that Florida's standards are world-class, that the FCAT or the Stanford-9 is challenging, or that the state of Florida's cut-scores represent performance at the levels of top-performing countries.

For whom are schools in Florida accountable? Virtually all students must take the state tests. The state excludes non-English-speaking students with fewer than two years of English-as-a-second-language instruction but tests those with more than two years of such instruction. On the other hand, the state allows non-English-speaking students who are tested to have extra time to divide the test into shorter testing periods or to have the teacher read questions out loud, or combinations of these accommodations. Some learning-disabled students may also be exempted, and those learning-disabled students who do take the test are given a modified form.

Is progress measured absolutely or relatively? Thus far, Florida has measured student progress in terms of reaching target scores that correspond to achievement levels. However, when Florida's value-added measurement system is in place, the state will be able to track relative gains made by teachers, schools, and districts.

Is Florida's accountability system fair? The state breaks down performance data into subgroups (economically disadvantaged, African American, white, Hispanic, Asian, and American Indian). In A or B schools, no subgroup can perform below the minimum criteria. However, Florida does not require that subgroups perform at a certain level in order for a school to receive a C grade (unlike Texas, which

---

[80]Ibid., 6.

requires that a certain percentage of each subgroup perform at a set level for the school to obtain an Acceptable rating).

Furthermore, the exit voucher option for students at failing schools allows some students from poor households to escape from a failing public school to a better-performing private school. Parents of most of these students could not usually afford to send them to private schools.

Is Florida's system informative? The state distributes individual student scores and the data on school report cards to districts, schools, and parents. State and district data are available on the Internet. It will be interesting to see, once value-added measurement is adopted, whether Florida will distribute information on individual teacher performance to parents. In Tennessee, where value-added analysis is part of that state's accountability system, the state provides value-added information on individual teacher performance only to school officials and to the teachers themselves.

What about rewards and sanctions in Florida? On the reward side, the state's merit-pay system is the most promising feature. Teachers' unions have fought merit pay across the country. If Florida's merit-pay system proves successful, it could be an example that inspires similar programs in other states and districts. Perhaps even more important, if value-added analysis is folded into the system, then Florida's merit-pay program would be based on an objective indicator of individual teacher performance and would give individual teachers incentive to improve their teaching and focus on teaching methods that actually increase student achievement.

On the sanctions side, the exit voucher option has fostered the most controversy but offers the most promise. Although few students have become eligible for the state-funded exit vouchers, there appears to be a positive "voucher effect" on the performance of failing public schools. In his analysis of A-Plus's exit voucher program, Greene found that "schools that received F grades in 1999 experienced increases in test scores that were more than twice as large as those experienced by schools with higher state-assigned grades."[81] The implication, of course, is that schools threatened with vouchers worked harder to improve their performance.

In response to the counterargument that the gains at failing schools had causes other than the prospect of vouchers, Greene compared higher-scoring F schools and lower-scoring D schools. He found that the F schools made higher gains than the D schools. Greene observed that "Given that the higher-scoring F schools were very much like the lower-scoring D schools, the fact that those schools that faced the prospect of vouchers made larger gains suggest that vouchers provide especially strong incentives to public schools to improve."[82]

Greene says that two forces are working to motivate schools to improve. First, all schools want to avoid the embarrassment of poor FCAT scores. But, said Greene, "schools with F scores had a second and very strong incentive to improve to avoid vouchers."[83] That incentive, according to Greene, was the prospect of market competition:

> Companies typically anticipate competitive threats and attempt to make appropriate responses to retain their customers before competition fully materializes. Similarly, it appears as if Florida schools that foresee the imminent challenge of having to compete for their students take the necessary steps to retain their students and stave off that competition.[84]

Concrete steps taken by local school officials have included implementing traditional teaching methods (such as direct instruction and drill and practice) in Lake County, switching to a phonics-reading program in Miami-Dade County, and requiring Saturday tutoring in Broward County. A report co-sponsored by the Miami Urban League

---

[81]Ibid.
[82]Ibid., 8.
[83]Ibid., 11.
[84]Ibid., 8–9.

and several think tanks observed that "the important thing is that the [exit voucher program] has instilled in the public schools a sense of urgency and zeal for reform not seen in the past when a school's failure was rewarded only with more money that reinforced failure."[85]

Greene, however, cautions that the A-Plus program is still new and that it may change for better or worse in the future. So far, students at only two schools have received exit vouchers. If the number of students eligible for the vouchers does not grow in the future, Greene warns that "it is possible that the prospect of having vouchers offered to students will not seem so imminent to schools and they will not face the same incentives to improve."[86] Perhaps Florida's criteria for offering exit vouchers should be more inclusive to allow more students the possibility of receiving them, thus keeping up the pressure on public schools to improve.[87]

Compared to California and Texas, Florida's accountability system includes programs that offer better incentives for schools and school personnel to reform their ineffective ways and to improve student achievement. It will be up to Florida policymakers to follow up on the state's promising beginning and to not lose sight of the principles and goals that put the system on the cutting edge of the accountability movement.

CONCLUSION

Despite the holes in many accountability systems, it is important not to lose perspective. Even under a less-than-optimal

---

[85]As cited in Lance T. Izumi, "School Choice Improves Public Schools," Pacific Research Institute for Public Policy, *Capital Ideas*, vol. 5, no. 43, October 25, 2000.

[86]Jay P. Greene, op. cit., 9.

[87]The December 2001 changes in the state's system of grading schools were brand-new at the time this was written, and their precise effects were unknown.

accountability system, the situation is often much better than when no accountability system existed. Not long ago, for example, California had no statewide assessment, had no sanctions for poor-performing schools, and paid little attention to improving student achievement. California's accountability system has focused the attention of adults in the public school system—from teachers to principals to superintendents to local and state policymakers—on the priority of raising student performance. Because of that attention, better curricula have been adopted, better teaching methods are entering the classroom, and pragmatism about what works is replacing faddish ideologies.

Nonetheless, there is much room for improvement. In California, too many low-performing schools are not subject to sanctions. In Texas, a state test that has not been challenging enough may have allowed too many schools to escape sanctions. In Florida, the voucher sanction may not apply to enough schools. State officials and accountability advocates must address these and many other problems if accountability systems are to reach their full potential.

The principles of a democratic society include responsibility on the part of public servants. In a democratic society, public institutions, including public schools, must be accountable for their results. Only when citizens can find out how their tax dollars are being used are they in a good position to demand change. Although serious accountability in public schools is only in its infancy, the movements in this direction across the country are encouraging. After decades of promises, we will now have incentives and accountability that can bring real improvement in student achievement.

ABBREVIATIONS

FCAT................................Florida Comprehensive Assessment Test
HSCAT......................High School Competency Assessment Test
(State of Florida)
HSEE..............High School Exit Examination (State of California)

ITBS.....................................Iowa Test of Basic Skills (Riverside)
NAEP.......................National Assessment of Educational Progress
Stanford-9.............Stanford Achievement Test, 9th ed. (Harcourt)
TAAS...................................Texas Assessment of Academic Skills
TAKS..........................Texas Assessment of Knowledge and Skills

Principles for Accountability Designs

Herbert J. Walberg

This chapter describes and illustrates a dozen design principles for school district, school, staff, and student accountability. Although many policymakers and analysts would agree with the need for accountability, the means are neither obvious nor agreed upon. Moreover, technical problems abound, including the lack of universal achievement scales, the matching of achievement tests to goals and standards, the scaling and expression of test scores, and the causal attribution of success to district central-office staff, principals, teachers, parents, and student socioeconomic background and effort.

Yet perfection is the enemy of steady improvement. States, foundations, and districts have made progress in solving these problems. They provide examples of principles that may reasonably be incorporated into accountability systems. Recent test scores for schools, for example, may be compared with their previous scores or those of comparable schools, or they may be statistically equated for fairer comparisons such as value-added metrics, which take into account previous tests scores, student demographic characteristics, and other factors. They may be reported in ways that are readily comprehensible to parents, the public, and legislators.

Well-defined standards can play a central role in accountability. By using them, school progress can be gauged according to the percentage of students that attain various levels such as the National Assessment Governing Board's Basic, Proficient, and Advanced levels for various subjects and grade levels.

Various difficulties, however, can arise: Standards may be too general or detailed, too difficult or easy, or too many or few. Similarly, tests may be difficult to construct. If employed for high-stakes decisions, a test may serve well for the first administration only but require new tests each year, which would result in difficult calibration with old tests to measure progress. Teachers may teach more exclusively to only that subject matter represented on the tests. Finally, it may take time to design curricular materials, lessons, and tests that best reflect the standards.

Even so, various states, foundations, and districts are solving these and other problems. As they gain more experience, they and others can review their progress, improve their programs, anticipate difficulties, and avoid them. This chapter draws upon the experience of such states and districts and sets forth implications for further improvement.

DESIGN PRINCIPLES

Authorities have written many books on accounting, auditing, various aspects of board-management and management-labor relations, and related topics. Accountability in education is far less mature, agreed-upon, and explicit. Yet some principles can be set forth to guide the development of K–12 school accountability systems that have proven workable in education practice. They are set forth in this section, and real-world examples are given in the next section.

A. General Principles

Dictionaries emphasize accountability as liability for being called into account or answerable for an explanation. Either meaning implies at least two sets of actors—those being called into account and those doing the calling, for example, management and labor, and parents and children. Schools, however, have a long and complex chain of accountability— citizens who elect their legislators to represent their interests, appointed or elected state school board officials and super-intendents, local boards, superintendents, and central office staff, principals, teachers, and students. It might be useful to think of each group as accountable to its predecessor in this list.

This linear accountability, however, is oversimplified, since, for example, federal regulations, high school depart-ment heads, other system employees, business influences, and others may require consideration. Superintendents may be accountable to the public as well as to teachers, other profes-sionals to their professional associations, students to their peers as well as to parents and teachers, and so on. Still, the important point is to recognize at least the two actors, one ac-countable to the other. Given this recognition, what princi-ples make for effective accountability?

1. Independence

In evaluating superintendents, school boards cannot rely completely upon their chief executive officer to provide accu-rate information. In addition to the superintendent's views and information, they should seek by formal and informal means the input of citizens, parents, teachers, auditors, and other third parties. Tests, community surveys, and public hearings are some formal means to complement official board reports and board members' impressions from informal ob-servations. Similarly, legislatures, state boards, and other groups should acquire or require independent information in addition to that routinely reported by those held accountable.

2. Focus on Results

Groups responsible for accountability routinely possess and discuss information on inputs but often are less well informed about results. For example, school boards routinely discuss finance, spending, class size, and staffing, among other things, but they appear less knowledgeable about where their students stand with respect to standards and rankings against similar or nearby districts and schools. Even educators themselves often have little technical mastery of psychometrics and statistics that would allow them to critically evaluate their students' progress.

3. User Friendliness

Readily understood reporting is desirable. Perhaps even a single number or two may best serve ocasionally. Many colleges, for example, want only two test scores and an applicant's high school grade-point average in making admission decisions. Stockholders and potential investors may first want to know the profit and increase in earnings, then the basis of the calculations, and then other organized numerical and verbal information.

What isn't as useful is a mass of undigested numbers often reported by states and districts in large, unwieldy books of computer printouts. A better system, exemplified in a subsequent section, allows school board members, educators, parents, and other interested parties, even those without technical experience, to design and execute within a few minutes reports with the comparisons and degree of detail they wish. They may then publish the report, and any comments they wish to make, on the Internet.

4. Timeliness

When I served as chair of the Design and Analysis Committee of the National Assessment Governing Board, it took the test vendor about sixteen months following the test administration to release the results. School boards and teachers often get test results long after their time of prime usefulness, namely, immediately. Large, national business firms usually report quarterly results, but some are capable of aggregating daily sales figures. One mark of a good teacher is getting test results back the next day. Boards, educators, firms, and others need rapid turnaround to make results useful.

The near future looks bright for timely results. Apparently, more than 100 firms are now working on computerized tests administered on the Internet. Such tests can be scored in several seconds; they save printing and mailing costs, can be quickly updated, and may require as few as a third of the testing time and items as the usual tests because they adapt the difficulty of the items to the students' ability, which is better estimated with each successive item. Open to the public, parents and students, independent of schools, could check their progress on demand in any given subject.

5. Incentives

Simply publishing results appears insufficient for progress. People and groups responsible for accountability should be able to offer incentives and sanctions for performance. Praise and recognition may go a long way, but money talks. The prospect of being hanged in the morning, wrote Samuel Johnson, concentrates the mind. There is much interest in superintendent bonuses for results, "merit pay" for teachers, and even payments to students. Schools have been closed for repeated failure; more students are being held back a grade because they haven't met standards. Schools of choice risk closing if they attract no students. Analogous thinking dominates much of the rest of society. Why not schools?

B. Examination Principles

As pointed out above, outcome information should be central for accountability, and test results provide the best indicators in several respects. Because multiple-choice tests are increasingly used for this purpose, and because many theorists, educators, and even psychometrists have criticized them, this section offers reasons why they should prevail.

1. Objectivity

Subjective impressions and reports about student work may be valuable, but they cannot be substituted for objective information, particularly quantified information. The most efficient, and perhaps most objective, indicators of outcomes are results on multiple-choice examinations because they are relatively cheap and require little subjectivity. Though useful for teachers in evaluating students' classroom work, essay examinations, laboratory exercises, oral reports, and similar "authentic examinations" are often highly subjective and lack technical adequacy, and they usually add very little information to what can be quickly assessed with objective procedures.[1]

2. Fairness

Objectively scored, often machine-scored, multiple-choice tests can be the fairest of all examinations in several senses. Teachers may be biased for or against some of their students. They may favor their own students or those of fellow teachers when results have high stakes. For this reason, other countries remove identification information from high-stakes examinations and employ teachers other than the students' own to make examinations fair.[2]

Multiple-choice tests are fair and defensible in another sense. In a small amount of time, they can sample a variety of parts of the subject matter and a range of "cognitive processes" from factual knowledge to "higher-order skills," such as analysis and synthesis. In contrast, a single essay question given in the same amount of time may arbitrarily give a huge advantage or disadvantage to a student, depending on whether or not an individual student had concentrated

---

[1]Herbert J.Walberg, Geneva D. Haertel, and Suzanne Gerlach-Downie, *Assessment Reform: Challenges and Opportunities,* Bloomington, IN: Phi Delta Kappa, 1994.

[2]John H. Bishop, "The Impact of Curriculum-Based External Examinations on School Priorities and Student Learning," *International Journal of Educational Research,* vol. 23, no. 8, 1996: 653–752.

study on the particular subtopic. A single essay question, moreover, can easily "leak out," and students who happen to find out may have an unfair advantage. Good writers who actually haven't mastered the subject matter can overly impress some graders. Although essay examinations, laboratory exercises, and problem solving should have a major place in the classroom, they often entail special difficulties in large-scale accountability systems.

3. Value-Added

Students who achieve well one year are likely to do well the next (and the likelihood increases with age). The same is true of schools, districts, and states. Further, how well they do is substantially determined by socioeconomic status and related factors, but schooling is another cause. To indicate the school's contribution to achievement, we can calculate value-added scores by subtracting the percentage of students attaining a given score or standard this year from last year's percentage.[3] Policymakers increasingly recognize that value-added scores better indicate the school's or teacher's contribution to achievement than do test scores at a single point in time. The apparent success of suburban schools, for example, may be substantially attributable to their socioeconomic composition rather than their efficiency.

Unadjusted, non-value-added scores, however, can complement value-added scores, and together they give policymakers more information and are less misleading than either one alone. For some purposes, moreover, status scores can serve alone. If schools are similar in socioeconomic and other

---

[3]Other ways to make value-added calculations are more complex, such as achievement residuals from regressions on previous scores, socioeconomic status indicators, and other measures, possibly for separate groups. In employing regression, mixed models, and their variants, we give up transparency or comprehensibility, especially to citizens who pay for schools. We also put ourselves in the hands of statistical experts who may agree that everything employed or proposed is defective but can agree on little else. Is it worth it?

advantages, they may be more validly compared on status. Nearby districts and schools may be of great interest to boards and parents, which may increase interest and justification of status scores. Some theorists and educators say that all children can learn to the same degree. Though value-added scores may best measure the progress of children or schools most in need of catching up, their ultimate interest should be status scores.

4. Balance

Balanced accountability systems require tests of multiple subjects, including science, history, geography, civics, and other subjects rather than the usual mathematics and reading tests alone, even though we may consider reading and mathematics to be foundational and pervasive. Boards need to consider ways to weigh or otherwise combine scores for an overall accountability index as well as providing desired detail.

Though multiple-choice tests are exceedingly efficient and cheap compared to other parts of educational programs, educators and students may face a considerable amount of testing, including the National Assessment of Educational Progress tests, national commercial tests, and state tests as well as special district, school, and frequent classroom tests. Some duplication of subject matter assessment may be desirable, but responsible boards and educators need to think through the entire testing program.

5. Score Expression

Scores on tests may be reported in a variety of ways such as percentiles and normal-curve equivalents. Because they are readily understood, methods of estimating the percentages of students attaining a given judgmental standard (or a national percentile such as the fiftieth or ninetieth) are gaining considerable ground. Still, such simple, concise indexes may cause distortions in educational programs. Strong incentives for getting the maximum number of students past, say, the fiftieth percentile may cause educators to neglect students who can easily pass this threshold and those who have little chance to make the cut. For this reason, the average of all students may be a better single representation of either status or progress.

It may be useful also to examine the percentages of students attaining quartiles or judgmental standards such as the National Assessment Governing Board's Basic, Proficient, and Advanced levels. Such detailed reporting allows a better understanding of where progress is and is not being made.

6. Disaggregation

The National Assessment of Educational Progress (NAEP) and some states and districts report the scores of boys and girls; African American, Hispanic, and white students; and poverty and nonpoverty students separately, thereby allowing a detailed review of each group's progress. The differences among these groups have also been reported as "the race gap" and "the poverty gap." Like quartile and multiple-standards reporting, such indexes allow close analysis of status and progress. In cases of sampling such as NAEP, however, small sample sizes may result in inaccurate estimates of the subpopulation figures.

7. Supplementary Opinion Surveys

Because examinations cannot capture all outcomes of schooling, supplementary information is useful. In principle, elected school board members represent the interests or views of their constituents, which they glean from daily life in the community and in special hearings. But surveys provide systematic evidence about changing views in their communities. Freely given information on possibly discrepant views of staff, parents, and students may give them a better understanding of the schools' problems and possible solutions. Public Agenda and Business Roundtable surveys, for example, show that the public, parents, teachers, and students support accountability and agree on the need for more rigorous standards.[4]

PRINCIPLES IN PRACTICE

Given the present state of accountability, the foregoing principles are somewhat idealistic. Yet we can consider successful instances of each in a limited number of districts and states, most of which I know from personal experience. This section discusses exemplary applications of the principles and illustrates them with actual accountability evidence.

A. CONSUMER-DESIGNED REPORTS

Available for California and Texas thus far, K–12Reports[5] is an Internet program that allows school board members, educators, parents, and citizens to analyze their school's, district's, or county's achievement standings. Without acquiring massive state databases and without spreadsheet skills, they can report scores in a variety of ways and publish comments on their findings. This section illustrates the displays an interested user can generate after investing several minutes in learning how to specify analyses.

1. *California County, District, and School Ranks*
Table 1 shows the opening screen for California. The counties are sorted from highest to lowest according to reading scores. Marin County is highest, and Merced County is lowest. The weighted average for the state is lower than the median district due to the fact that Los Angeles County has many low-scoring students and the higher scoring districts tend to have smaller numbers of students. San Diego, Sacramento, and San Francisco counties score substantially higher than Los Angeles County.

---

[4]See the Internet sites <www.brt.org> and <www.publicagenda.org>.
[5]See Internet site <www.K-12Reports.com> for additional reports or to specify custom displays and to publish reports.

TABLE 1
Percentages of Students in All Grades Scoring At or Above the Fiftieth National Percentile on the Stanford Achievement Test, Spring 2000

County	Reading	Math	Language	Spelling
Marin	**73.7**	**76.9**	77.3	**65.9**
Nevada	65.2	70.2	66.3	54.3
Placer	64.6	68.2	68.0	60.5
El Dorado	62.7	66.7	65.9	54.5
Amador	60.9	61.2	63.9	53.0
San Luis Obispo	60.4	66.6	65.3	53.7
Tuolumne	58.8	61.9	60.3	49.9
Sonoma	57.7	60.7	62.0	50.9
Mariposa	57.5	63.3	61.0	47.9
Calaveras	56.6	56.6	57.6	46.3
Humboldt	56.5	59.5	58.6	48.3
Trinity	56.5	61.8	56.4	46.7
Plumas	56.0	56.9	57.6	50.8
Alpine	55.2	61.2	55.9	45.6
Sierra	55.0	59.5	58.7	50.5
Contra Costa	54.9	59.8	59.7	55.6
Santa Clara	54.0	63.1	61.6	56.5
Mono	53.9	56.5	59.2	45.4
San Mateo	53.8	60.2	61.0	56.5
Siskiyou	52.8	58.6	53.8	43.0
Ventura	52.4	58.4	59.0	51.6
Lassen	51.6	56.4	52.3	43.9
Inyo	50.5	55.2	52.9	43.0
Yolo	50.4	56.5	54.6	46.9
San Diego	**50.3**	**59.4**	**56.6**	**50.8**
Shasta	**50.3**	**56.2**	**53.0**	**46.7**
Napa	50.3	57.8	55.7	43.4
Orange	49.5	60.2	57.8	52.1
Alameda	48.9	55.7	55.7	50.6

continued on next page

TABLE 1 (*continued*)

County	Reading	Math	Language	Spelling
Solano	48.2	53.8	53.8	50.3
Butte	47.7	52.0	51.9	40.6
Santa Barbara	47.6	55.0	53.2	45.8
Sacramento	**47.4**	**53.5**	**52.9**	**50.6**
San Francisco	**46.9**	**60.1**	**56.4**	**54.6**
Santa Cruz	46.6	53.2	50.1	39.1
Tehama	46.5	53.9	48.2	41.2
Modoc	46.5	55.2	49.8	42.2
Mendocino	**45.9**	**49.6**	**49.3**	**37.8**
Del Norte	44.2	53.4	48.1	41.0
Stanislaus	43.4	52.1	49.0	42.1
Lake	**43.2**	**48.2**	**46.7**	**36.7**
California	**43.1**	**51.2**	**49.9**	**44.7**
San Benito	**41.9**	**48.9**	**45.5**	**38.3**
Sutter	41.2	49.6	47.1	39.7
Glenn	40.6	47.3	46.0	41.6
Riverside	39.5	48.0	46.4	40.1
Yuba	39.1	44.2	43.5	39.3
San Bernardino	37.4	45.4	45.0	39.5
San Joaquin	36.8	45.6	45.0	40.1
Fresno	36.5	45.9	43.0	39.4
Kern	36.2	45.0	42.8	39.8
Madera	35.7	45.6	41.4	36.6
Kings	35.0	39.3	40.6	37.7
Los Angeles	**34.4**	**43.3**	**43.1**	**39.1**
Monterey	34.0	41.2	40.1	33.4
Tulare	30.9	40.4	37.6	31.0
Imperial	29.5	39.8	38.9	36.5
Colusa	29.3	40.6	35.7	30.5
Merced	**29.0**	**39.6**	**37.5**	**31.1**

Note: Counties referred to in the text are bolded.

On the Internet version of the table, clicking on the italicized words at the top of the table (URLs, or "universal resource locators," in Internet jargon) sorts in several seconds the counties by another subject. Clicking on any county in the left column displays the similarly ranked district scores within the county. Clicking then on any district URL displays the ranked schools within the district. With an additional click, county, district, and schools can be ranked by means or twenty-fifth, fiftieth, and seventy-fifth quartiles on any subject for all grades together or for separate grades.

The schools can also readily be ranked by an index of value added, that is, in this case, the percentage difference between any grade and the previous grade. From the second to the third grade, for example, only four of the fifty-eight counties in the table, San Benito, Mendocino, Shasta, and Lakes, showed gains in the percentages of students at or above the fiftieth percentile. In the state as a whole, 5 percent fewer third than second graders met this national criterion. For the 4,078,575 students with reading data in the state, the average drop in percentage attaining the fiftieth national percentile is 1.4 percent per grade level, suggesting that the longer students are in California schools, the worse their national rank.

2. California Poverty-Gap Analysis

In addition to analyzing the scores of all students, K–12Reports can rank the scores of the following groups within the state, counties, and districts:

- Limited English Proficient, non-LEP, and the difference between them

- Boys, girls, and the difference between them

- Special and nonspecial education students and the difference between them

- Economically advantaged, disadvantaged students, and the difference between them

As an example, Table 2 illustrates the differences among California counties with respect to the poverty gap (or difference between Title 1 and other students). Illustrating the pervasive effects of poverty, every district shows a gap. But the range of differences is huge: In contrast to San Francisco County, San Diego and Sacramento counties have huge poverty gaps. Humboldt, Nevada, Del Norte, and Sierra counties have the smallest gaps, and Marin County has the biggest poverty gap. The service enables users to "drill down" to examine which districts, schools, and grades do well not only on average but also with respect to gaps and reducing gaps among groups from one grade to the next.

Educators and others can also post comments and questions about the tables. They may, for example, venture hypotheses about the results, provoke further analyses, and suggest constructive actions based on evidence selected and analyzed in accordance with their concerns. They can engage in dialogues with others who can readily publish other analyses and commentary on the publicly available Internet.

Thus, K–12Reports illustrates several of the design principles discussed in the previous section, including user friendliness, independent analysis, focus on results, timeliness, value added, comprehensiveness, score expression, and disaggregation. It might be argued also that such readily executable and publicly publishable reports will lead to greater use of incentives for superintendents, principals, and other educators because they provide a better basis of evidence than do underanalyzed data, which are less accessible and analyzable by the public, parents, and legislators.

B. Exemplary District Accountability

Most districts around the country employ a variety of national, state, and district tests. Even so, they rarely analyze tests in ways that are optimally suited for accountability. Though typical in this respect, tiny Butler District 53 in Oak Brook, Illinois, a western suburb of Chicago, is distinctive in

TABLE 2
Gap in Percentages between Advantaged and Disadvantaged Eighth Grade Students At or Above the Fiftieth National Percentile on the Stanford Achievement Test, Spring 2000

County	Reading	Math	Language	Spelling
Marin	54	48	51	43
Santa Cruz	47	37	41	31
Contra Costa	43	42	40	30
Fresno	42	35	37	27
San Mateo	42	32	35	29
Madera	41	38	37	23
Orange	41	37	36	31
Ventura	40	37	37	32
Santa Barbara	40	33	35	30
Tulare	38	29	34	25
Napa	37	31	38	29
Kern	37	30	33	24
San Diego	37	35	35	28
Sacramento	36	29	34	24
San Benito	36	27	36	22
Sonoma	36	27	36	25
Monterey	36	31	31	28
California	36	32	32	27
Santa Clara	36	31	33	29
Colusa	36	31	39	33
Alameda	34	28	31	23
Imperial	33	28	32	28
Sutter	33	30	31	18
Los Angeles	33	30	30	27
Glenn	33	19	24	19
San Luis Obispo	33	31	32	27
Yolo	33	30	30	24
Modoc	32	35	32	23

continued on next page

TABLE 2 (*continued*)

County	Reading	Math	Language	Spelling
Butte	32	28	29	18
Inyo	32	33	26	19
San Joaquin	31	25	28	18
Amador	31	33	16	17
Merced	31	21	24	17
San Bernardino	30	27	27	20
Stanislaus	29	20	24	19
Lake	28	28	25	12
Riverside	28	26	26	20
Kings	26	19	25	18
Lassen	26	30	20	18
Mariposa	26	16	16	16
Mendocino	25	25	25	18
Solano	25	20	25	19
Siskiyou	25	14	17	8
Calaveras	24	17	22	16
Tehama	24	20	19	8
Yuba	23	16	19	11
Tuolumne	23	18	15	20
Placer	23	21	20	18
Plumas	23	21	19	7
El Dorado	23	25	23	20
Shasta	23	26	23	18
Mono	23	32	23	15
Trinity	21	21	26	14
San Francisco	**19**	**7**	**16**	**15**
Humboldt	**18**	**14**	**17**	**8**
Nevada	**14**	**20**	**18**	**16**
Del Norte	**10**	**5**	**8**	**10**
Sierra	**1**	**−1**	**12**	**27**

Note: Counties referred to in the text are boldface.

being one of the highest spending districts in Illinois and one of the most affluent areas in the country.

By several measures, Butler students appeared to rank far less well than might be expected from spending and economic status. The board wanted a long-term accountability design, an initial assessment of all available data, and a plan to compensate the superintendent for future accomplishments. The board appointed two of its members, the administrative staff, and a consultant to carry out these tasks. The initial report further exemplifies several of the design principles described in the previous section and illustrated below.

1. National Standings

The EXPLORE academic assessment yields achievement information to educators, parents, and students for high school and career planning. The following chart shows how Butler District eighth graders compared with national norms in seven subjects. As expected, the students were concentrated in the first quartile and very few scored below the fiftieth percentile.

The chart also illustrates a common pattern among test data for students, schools, and districts: Contrary to the common assumption, those who do well on one test usually do well on others.

2. Value-Added Analysis

The California statewide, value-added analysis described in the previous section employed "synthetic cohort . . . raw gains," that is, the simple differences in means at a single point in time between one grade and the previous grade. Other things being equal, more complex analyses can be advantageous, especially in tracing individual students over one or more years.[6] Employed in the Butler District is SAS in School, led by William Saunders, who first gained national prominence for such analyses in Tennessee. Data were available for

---

[6]Experts lack agreement on the best way to calculate these, and the basis and method of some calculations are not completely explicit. Such scores lack transparency and comprehensibility for all but a few people with specialized technical skills.

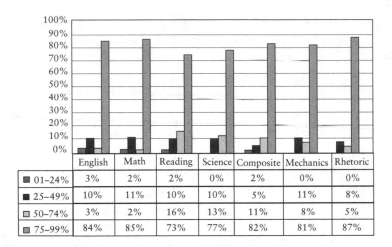

	English	Math	Reading	Science	Composite	Mechanics	Rhetoric
■ 01–24%	3%	2%	2%	0%	2%	0%	0%
■ 25–49%	10%	11%	10%	10%	5%	11%	8%
□ 50–74%	3%	2%	16%	13%	11%	8%	5%
▨ 75–99%	84%	85%	73%	77%	82%	81%	87%

Butler District Assessment

the last three years in nine subjects from California Test Bureau/McGraw-Hill's California Achievement Test data. Grades 2, 4, and 8 could not be computed because test score gains were not available for the three most recent years.

The next table provides a compact summary of the SAS in School results by subject for the years 1997 through 2000. As on traffic lights, a green or favorable light is represented by G. Similarly, yellow (Y) suggests caution and red (R) suggests stopping for a closer examination. Ultra-Red, or R*, suggests value-added gains considerably below those of other schools in the United States.

Because affluent districts score better than state and national averages (often attributable to socioeconomic factors), few or perhaps none have undergone rigorous value-added analysis. For the Butler District, the grade 3 results are mixed, grade 5 made progress in five of ten instances, grade 6 in eight of twelve instances (though its performance was distinctly below the national average in two cases (R*)), and grade 7 made good progress in nine of twelve instances.

In sum, Butler District 53 students made better than national progress in twenty-two, or 61 percent, of thirty-six

Subject	2	3	4	5	6	7	8
Language Total				G	G	G	
Math Total				G	G	G	
Reading Total				Y	G	G	
Science		G			G	G	
Social Studies		R			R*	G	
Language Expression				Y	G	G	
Language Mechanics				G	G	G	
Math Computation				Y	G	Y	
Math Concepts and Applications				G	R	Y	
Reading Comprehension				R	G	G	
Reading Vocabulary				Y	Y	G	
Spelling				G	R*	Y	

SAS in Schools

instances during the most recent three-year period. Caution is indicated in 22 percent of the instances. A closer examination is suggested in 8 percent of the cases, and performance is considerably below that of other schools in 6 percent of the instances. This analysis suggests more urgent priorities than the status results almost universally reported and exemplified in the previous chart.

3. Student Progress by Initial Test Score

The next table summarizes progress in grades 3 through 8 for students in five national quintiles during the previous year. Though some statisticians may prefer a three-year assessment of schools, grades, or teachers, their preference or insistence trades immediacy for accuracy. A teacher may, for example, be rapidly declining from excellent to poor to unacceptable, but a rolling three-year average may not signal a sharp warning until the end of the fourth or fifth year, in which case children would have suffered a severe multiple-year setback. So the three-year preference is merely a trade-off to be made by responsible agents such as conscientious board members

Subject	1 Lowest	2	3 Middle	4	5 Highest
Language Total	++++	+++	++++	++++	+++++
Mathematics Total	+++++	+++	++++	+++	++++
Reading Total	+++	++++	++++	++++	+++
Science	++++	++++	++++	++++	++++
Social Studies	++++	+++	+	++	++
Language Expression	+++++	+++++	+++++	+++	++++
Language Mechanics	++++	+++	++	++++	++++
Math Computation	+	++	+++	+++	+++
Math Concepts and Applications	+++++	++++	++++	++++	+++++
Reading Comprehension	+	++++	+++	+++	++++
Reading Vocabulary	+++++	++++	++++	++	+++
Spelling	+++	+	++	+++	+++

Progress

rather than on moral or "high science" grounds. In addition, teachers who excel in the past year should hear about it and be rewarded quickly, even if the value-added gain measure is somewhat less precise than a three-year or career average.

In any case, each plus in the table indicates that one grade made better than average national progress. The fifth, or highest, quintile under Language Total, for example, has five pluses, which indicates that students in this quintile made better-than-average progress in five of the six grades.

The chart shows that by this criterion Butler students performed well: In more than two-thirds of the cases (207 out of 300), their progress exceeded the nation's. Progress was especially consistent in Science, Language Expression, and Math Concepts and Applications, with twenty or more pluses across quintiles. Except perhaps for the lowest quintile in Math Computation and Reading Comprehension, there was little tendency for top, bottom, or middle quintile students to make greater progress than other students in the district. Still, progress was only average or less than the nation's in Mathematics Computation and Spelling in half or less than half the grades. A board member might ask why there wasn't above-average performance in every subject in every grade. She might also ask for the specific results for each teacher.

4. Grade-Level Analysis

The data discussed in a previous section show that the longer California students are in school, the more likely they are to be below the national median. The percentage above the median in reading, for example, declined from 49 to 34; Language Arts declined from 52 to 40.

On the other hand, the Butler District 53 board had instituted a rigorous test published by the Educational Records Bureau (ERB), which is more often used in private and elite suburban schools, and wanted a similar indication of students' relative progress through the grades even though only one round of test data was available.

The next chart shows the median ERB percentile composite scores (Word Analysis, Reading Comprehension, Mathematics, Writing Mechanics, Verbal Ability, Vocabulary, and Quantitative Ability) for District 53, suburban schools, and independent schools. This chart shows that District 53 and the national sample of suburban schools can be found around the seventy-second percentile; they both generally pull further ahead of national norms with each higher grade. District 53, however, moved ahead faster and actually caught up with independent schools by eighth grade.

5. Peer District Comparison

Given Butler District 53's affluence and school spending, some parents and board members would not be content with exceeding other national samples of suburban schools and catching up with independent schools. Close to Oak Brook is Naperville, with claims for the best science and mathematics scores among elite suburban schools in the nation

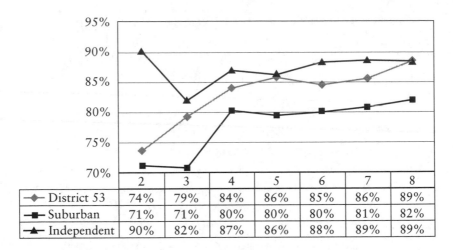

	2	3	4	5	6	7	8
District 53	74%	79%	84%	86%	85%	86%	89%
Suburban	71%	71%	80%	80%	80%	81%	82%
Independent	90%	82%	87%	86%	88%	89%	89%

Median Percentile Scores by Grade

when compared on the Third International Mathematics and Science Study examinations. The Illinois Standards Achievement Tests (ISAT) afforded a comparison of elite Chicago area suburban districts. Because Butler District 53 has only a primary and a middle school, the best-scoring school in each elite district was sampled using composite ISAT scores for reading, math, science, social science, and writing for such schools.

The next chart shows Butler 53 placed fifteenth out of twenty-five elite schools. The top-scoring Edison Elementary and Peoria are schools for gifted children. If these two are excluded, District 53 outperforms almost half the schools in this elite pool.

The foregoing analyses exemplify several design principles described in a preceding section, including value added, comprehensiveness, score expression, and disaggregation. They show that the usual assortment of various test data in school district files can be marshaled to give a fuller picture of the district's accomplishments and needs for improvement. From these and other analyses, the Butler District 53 board members felt confident in setting specific merit-pay goals for the superintendent.

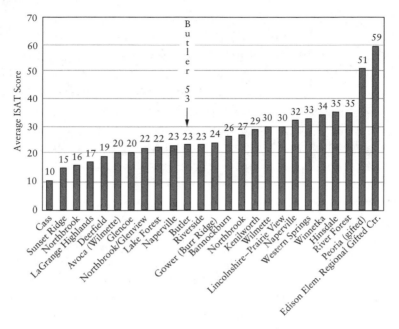

Year 2000 Average ISAT Performance by District

C. Student Accountability and Incentives

Just as much as educators, students need better accountability and more explicit incentives, as they themselves agree. A 1996 Public Agenda national survey of high school students showed that three-fourths believe that stiffer examinations and graduation requirements would make students pay more attention to their studies. Three-fourths also said students who have not mastered English should not graduate, and a similar percentage said schools should promote only students who master the material. Almost two-thirds reported they could do much better in school if they tried. Nearly 80 percent said students would learn more if schools made sure students were on time and did their homework. More than 70 percent said schools should require after-school classes for those earning Ds and Fs.[7]

---

[7]Herbert J. Walberg, "Incentivized School Standards Work," *Education Week,* November 4, 1998, p. 37.

1. Learning Consequences

Experimental research in the classrooms corroborates students' common sense and insight. Among dozens of teaching methods subject to meta-analysis (statistical syntheses of studies), frequent testing substantially benefits learning because it encourages students to be prepared and provides information on their progress to both students and teachers. Positive teacher feedback about students' good accomplishments is among the most powerful teaching methods.[8]

Surveys also provide support for better student accountability. In his classic 1961 study, *The Adolescent Society,* sociologist James Coleman showed how teenage concerns with cars, clothes, and dating precluded long, hard study.[9] Since then, television has taken a larger share of students' time and consumes nearly as many weekly hours as they spend in classes.

Economist John Bishop has long studied examination effects on learning. From large-scale survey data, he analyzed the effects of examinations of the (U.S.) Advanced Placement program, the New York State Regents, Canadian provinces, and European ministries. These examinations have the common elements of being externally composed and geared toward agreed-upon subject matter that students are to learn within a country, state, or province. They are often given at the end of relevant courses. Most important, they have substantial positive effects on learning.[10]

The largest, and most sophisticated, international comparative analysis of national achievement yet conducted corroborates Bishop's findings about constructive effects of

---

[8]Herbert J. Walberg, "Meta-Analytic Effects for Policy," in Gregory J. Cizek, editor, *Handbook of Educational Policy*, San Diego, CA: Academic Press, 1999, pp. 419–454.

[9]James S. Coleman, *The Adolescent Society,* New York: Free Press, 1961.

[10]John H. Bishop, "The Impact of Curriculum-Based External Examinations on School Priorities and Student Learning," *International Journal of Educational Research* 23 (8) (1996): 653–752.

external curriculum-based examinations.[11] America's lack of such exams, the short school year, and limited homework requirements are three of the major reasons why U.S. students come in last in value-added achievement gains.

On-the-ground anecdotal reports from experienced observers bear out the harm of slack accountability and even complicity. The title of Sizer's book *Horace's Compromise* conveys the too-frequently-implicit contract: teachers give good grades without academically challenging their students; students, in return, don't cause difficulty.[12]

Most economists and some psychologists subscribe to the idea that people rationally choose what they perceive maximizes their benefits and minimizes their costs and risks. Parents would like their children to work hard for future gains, but many adults are held accountable in their own lives, yearly, quarterly, and sometimes much more frequently as the appropriate occasions arise. Yet educators and parents seem to expect that their charges will work hard without feedback for vague, very long-term goals such as gaining entrance to a good college and enhancing their marital and career prospects. To children and teenagers such benefits may appear intangible, uncertain, and in the far distant future. High achievement, moreover, requires time and energies that could go into the pursuit of other fascinating opportunities offered by their peer culture.

What would happen if they were challenged and incentivized? The O'Donnell Foundation of Dallas tried it out and asked me to study the program. The Foundation paid students $100 for each passing score on the Advanced Placement (AP) examinations in English, calculus, statistics, computer science, biology, chemistry, and physics, plus a reimbursement for the cost of taking the exam. The

---

[11]Ludger Woessmann, "Why Students in Some Countries Do Better," *Education Matters,* Summer 2001: 67–74.

[12]Theodore R. Sizer, *Horace's Compromise: The Dilemmas of the American High School,* Boston: Houghton-Mifflin, 1984.

program also provided a $2,500 stipend to each teacher undergoing training to teach advanced courses in those subjects. They also received $100 for each passing AP examination score of their students.

In the nine participating Dallas schools, sharply increasing numbers of boys and girls of all major ethnic groups took and passed the AP exams. The number rose more than twelve-fold, from 41 the year before the program began to 521 when it ended in 1994–95. After its termination, the program continued to have carry-over effects: In the 1996–97 school year, two years after the program ended, 442 students passed, about eleven times more than the number in the year before the program began. Despite education theory, incentives appear to work in schools as they do in other human activities.[13] To work, however, rigorous, clear standards and significant benefits are required. Otherwise, as some economists maintain, students would be irrational. If we think they are, we may not realize their perceived benefits and costs.

2. Student Accountability Benefits
In short, there is much consistent evidence that accountability and incentives work to improve achievement. Are there other benefits?

1. Higher achievement in high school also increases the probability of admission to college. During the past fifteen years, the payoff for college attendance has more than doubled. Higher achievers are also more often admitted into potentially lucrative majors such as engineering and premedicine. Higher achieving high school students tend not only to be admitted but to graduate from better colleges and to enter graduate and professional programs.

2. As measured on objective examinations, achievement in rigorous high school courses tends to be rewarded as better

---

[13]See Walberg, 1998, in the work cited previously.

pay for graduates. As Bishop points out, the premium employers pay for graduates with higher mathematics achievement has increased substantially. Front-line workers are increasingly assuming responsibility for functions formerly carried out by engineers and managers.

3. Higher achievement also has broader spillover effects. Parents and communities may derive honor and prestige from high-achieving youth. High achievers raise national income and contribute more to their local economies. They pay more taxes and, as informed voters and citizens, may raise the quality of civic and community life.

4. Achievement information yielded by better accountability systems would be valuable to employers to make better hiring decisions. To the extent that employers pay higher achievers more, they make their workforce more efficient and increase student incentives to do better. Relying on such information would help eliminate subjective racial, sexual, and other bias and the inconsistencies of interviews.[14]

5. Fostered in school, reading proficiency is also of huge economic and social significance. Bormuth's careful survey of about five thousand people aged sixteen and over showed that 87 percent of those employed reported that they had to read as part of their jobs. Typical working people read for 141 minutes per day as part of their jobs, or about 29 percent of the workday. Because the national wage bill in 1971 was $859 billion, Bormuth estimated that U.S. workers earned $253 billion for on-the-job reading. Because there are more workers today, because they undoubtedly read even more, and because their hourly wages have increased, the amount paid for on-the-job reading must be substantially greater today.[15] Arguably, U.S. citizens are paid more for reading than any other activity.

---

[14]See the work cited by Bishop for evidence and further arguments supporting the first four points.

[15]John R. Bormuth, "Value and Volume of Literacy," *Visible Language* 12 (1978): 118–161.

6. Accurate information on applicants would allow colleges to provide merit scholarships and allow advanced students to graduate early. In the 1950s, President Robert M. Hutchins of the University of Chicago designed a program to provide early admission to qualified high school students that allowed them to graduate as young as age eighteen. Many went on for graduate and professional degrees.

The results of less substantial, but carefully evaluated, recent programs show that qualified students allowed to skip to advanced courses learned far more than others who were similarly qualified. Enacted again, "Hutchins degree" programs would save students' time and allow them longer careers. Families and taxpayers would save money.

Grades, however, cannot provide the accurate, objective information required for all these purposes. Teachers vary enormously in what content they teach, the rigor of their examinations, and in their grading policies. About 80 percent of the questions on high school teachers' tests concern factual information rather than analysis, synthesis, and evaluation of ideas. Student ranks in their classes are no better because they are based on averages of grades.

Some high school students can pass examinations for advanced college work in ancient history, calculus, physics, and Japanese. Some college seniors cannot pass freshman high school examinations. American education lacks objective standards. Diplomas and degrees are awarded not for proficiency but for seat time.

Japan and most advanced Western countries employ examinations that overcome these comparability problems. Though there are variations in their design, the examinations are composed for courses in the arts, languages, and sciences offered in an entire nation, province, or state. Though the scope of each examination is well known, they are often graded or checked by educators other than the students' own teachers.

Because the exams and courses are uniform, teachers need not figure out what content to teach and subsequent teachers can depend on what students have been taught. It is useless for students to contest their teachers about standards because they are externally imposed. Rather, students and teachers become coworkers in trying to meet the standards.

CONCLUSION

Accountability works in schooling as it does in other constructive activities. Experience with accountability systems suggests a dozen accountability principles, including a focus on results, user friendliness, independent assessments, timeliness, and value-added indexes. As illustrated in this chapter, examples of their success can be found in states, districts, schools, and classrooms.

The present danger is letting the perfect defeat the better. The schooling establishment and its status quo defenders resist examinations, accountability, and standards because they claim they haven't been tried. As shown here, they have in fact been tried and found successful in this country and overseas. They are pervasive not only in sports and other leisure pursuits but in occupations and professions as well. The big accountability exception is American schooling, which may account for its poor and declining productivity and students' poor preparation for college, work, and citizenship.

Contributors

WILLIAMSON M. EVERS, research fellow at the Hoover Institution, serves on the National Educational Research Policy and Priorities Board. He also served as a commissioner of the California State Commission for the Establishment of Academic Content and Performance Standards and is a member of the panels writing mathematics and history questions for California's statewide testing system. He is the editor of *What's Gone Wrong in America's Classrooms* and the co-editor of *School Reform: The Critical Issues.*

CHESTER E. FINN, JR., is president of the Thomas B. Fordham Foundation and the John M. Olin Fellow at the Manhattan Institute. A professor of education and public policy at Vanderbilt University (on leave), he also served as Assistant Secretary for Research and Improvement and as Counselor to the Secretary of the U.S. Department of Education. With William J. Bennett and John Cribb, he recently authored *The Educated Child: A Parent's Guide From Preschool Through 8th Grade,* and he currently serves as the senior editor for *Education Next.*

ERIC A. HANUSHEK is the Paul and Jean Hanna Senior Fellow at the Hoover Institution. His works on education policy include *Improving America's Schools: The Role of Incentives, Making Schools Work: Improving Performance and Controlling Costs,* and *Educational Performance of the Poor: Lessons from Rural Northeast Brazil.* His current research involves understanding the role of teachers, programs, and funding in determining student achievement.

CAROLINE M. HOXBY is a professor of economics at Harvard University. She is the editor of the forthcoming book *The Economics of School Choice* and the author of several influential papers on education policy, including "Does Competition Among Public Schools Benefit Students and Taxpayers," "The Effects of Class Size and Composition on Student Achievement: New Evidence from Natural Population Variation," and "Not All School Finance Equalizations Are Created Equal."

LANCE T. IZUMI is a senior fellow in California Studies and the director of the Center for School Reform at the Pacific Research Institute. He is the author of *Facing the Classroom Challenge: Teacher Quality and Teacher Training in California's Schools of Education, California Index of Leading Education Indicators* (1997 and 2000 editions), *Developing and Implementing Academic Standards,* as well as many articles. He serves as a member of the California Postsecondary Education Commission and of the Professional Development Working Group of the California Legislature's Joint Committee to Develop a Master Plan for K–12 Education.

MARGARET E. RAYMOND is the director of CREDO, a research and evaluation component of the Hoover Institution. She recently completed the first evaluation of the effectiveness of the Teach for America program. Her current work involves a variety of policy analyses and evaluations of accountability systems and educational programs.

DIANE RAVITCH, research professor at New York University, holds the Brown Chair in Education Policy at the Brookings Institution. She is a member of the National Assessment Governing Board, to which she was appointed by Secretary of Education Richard Riley. From 1991 to 1993, she served as Assistant Secretary of Education and Counselor to Secretary of Education Lamar Alexander. A historian of American education, she is the author of many books, including *The Great School Wars*, *The Troubled Crusade*, and *Left Back: A Century of Failed School Reforms*.

HERBERT J. WALBERG, formerly research professor of education and psychology and now University Scholar at the University of Illinois at Chicago, has edited more than sixty books and written approximately 350 articles on educational productivity and human accomplishment. He is one of ten U.S. members of the International Academy of Education and a fellow of several scholarly associations in the U.S. and abroad.

Index